LITERARY PATHS TO RELIGIOUS UNDERSTANDING

Also by G. Douglas Atkins

The Faith of John Dryden: Change and Continuity (1980)

Reading Deconstruction/Deconstructive Reading (1983)—selected by *Choice* as "An Outstanding Academic Book" for 1984–85

Writing and Reading Differently: Deconstruction and the Teaching of Composition and Literature, co-edited with Michael L. Johnson (1985)

Quests of Difference: Reading Pope's Poems (1986)

Shakespeare and Deconstruction, co-edited with David M. Bergeron (1988)

Contemporary Critical Theory, co-edited with Laura Morrow (1988)

Geoffrey Hartman: Criticism as Answerable Style (1990)

Estranging the Familiar: Toward a Revitalized Critical Writing (1992)—selected by *Choice* as "An Outstanding Academic Book" for 1993–94

Tracing the Essay: Through Experience to Truth (2005)

Reading Essays: An Invitation (2008)

On the Familiar Essay: Challenging Academic Orthodoxies (2009)

T.S. Eliot and the Essay (forthcoming)

LITERARY PATHS TO RELIGIOUS UNDERSTANDING

ESSAYS ON DRYDEN, POPE, KEATS, GEORGE ELIOT, JOYCE, T.S. ELIOT, AND E.B. WHITE

G. Douglas Atkins

Parts of Chapter 5, "Journey toward Understanding: T.S. Eliot and the Progress of the 'Intelligent Believer,'" first appeared in *On the Familiar Essay: Challenging Academic Orthodoxies*, Palgrave Macmillan, October 2009. Used by permission.

First published in 2009 by
PALGRAVE MACMILLAN®
in the United States—a division of St. Martin's Press LLC,
175 Fifth Avenue, New York, NY 10010.

Where this book is distributed in the UK, Europe and the rest of the world, this is by Palgrave Macmillan, a division of Macmillan Publishers Limited, registered in England, company number 785998, of Houndmills, Basingstoke, Hampshire RG21 6XS.

Palgrave Macmillan is the global academic imprint of the above companies and has companies and representatives throughout the world.

Palgrave® and Macmillan® are registered trademarks in the United States, the United Kingdom, Europe and other countries.

ISBN: 978–0–230–62147–3

Library of Congress Cataloging-in-Publication Data

Atkins, G. Douglas (George Douglas), 1943–
    Literary paths to religious understanding : essays on Dryden, Pope, Keats, George Eliot, Joyce, T.S. Eliot, And E.B. White / G. Douglas Atkins.
        p. cm.
    ISBN 978–0–230–62147–3 (alk. paper)
    1. English literature—History and criticism. 2. Christianity and literature. 3. Christianity in literature. I. Title.

PR145.A75 2009
820.9'382—dc22   2009016315

A catalogue record of the book is available from the British Library.

Design by Newgen Imaging Systems (P) Ltd., Chennai, India.

First edition: December 2009

10 9 8 7 6 5 4 3 2 1

Printed in the United States of America.

In loving memory of my parents

CONTENTS

ACKNOWLEDGMENTS

My debts are, of course, many; they are also outstanding, and the mere mention of names here will not reduce my debt, nor should it. Without T.S. Eliot's writing, I might never have found out about Incarnation. Without Dr. Vincent Miller of Wofford College, I might never have found out about T.S. Eliot. I always think of my late parents, George and Thursey Mae, whose love was unconditional—I hope this book makes some amends for my choosing, so many years ago, a secular priesthood. I think, too, of the Rev. Henry (Hank) Keating, then associate minister of the First Presbyterian Church of Spartanburg, SC, who introduced me to theological study via a course at Converse College in 1965. I think as well of Dr. Matthew Stein, physician, humanist, who has more than once saved my life. I cannot fail to mention Millie Atkins, née Bowfort Black-and-Bonnie, the Cavalier King Charles Spaniel who keeps me Anglicized and who has taught me so much about love. Also, my daughter Leslie, her husband Craig, and their daughter Kate and my son Christopher, his wife Sharon, and their son Oliver—they all make me proud, and I love them unreservedly, as I do my wife Rebecca Lynn, Millie's mother, who, with me now in Kansas, yokes together Maine and South Carolina. I must also and gladly acknowledge my debt to the superior folks at Palgrave Macmillan, especially Erin Ivy, Brigitte Shull, and Lee Norton. I thank, finally, Palgrave's readers of my manuscript, who helped make this a much better book (and who don't bear any responsibility for problems that remain).

An earlier, quite different version of chapter 2 appeared as "*The Eve of St. Agnes* Reconsidered," *Tennessee Studies in Literature* 18 (1973), 113–32.

PREFATORY ESSAY

The relation of literature and religion since the Protestant Reformation has been troubled, to say the least. The clergy has often been critical and disparaging of the observations, reflections, and dramatizations of poets and writers, who have "progressed" from more or less rabid anticlericalism to laments and proclamations about "the disappearance," "the absence," more recently "the death" of God, and currently His (or Her) virtual and practical irrelevance. Although signs appear of renewed interest in religion, even among scholars, I do not sense the fervor of the mid-twentieth century when critics such as J. Hillis Miller, following upon the earlier works of T.S. Eliot and some others, were examining literature and religion together, nor of the excitement and turmoil of the 1970s and 1980s, when I penned "A(fter) D(econstruction): Literature and Religion in the Wake of Deconstruction" and "Dehellenizing Literary Criticism."[1] Criticism has not, in any case, been revitalized, and religion appears to have borne the slashing waves of fashion and prosperity no better than deconstruction. No one, then, or now, has paid much attention to the precise nature of the *relation* between literature and religion.

Nowadays Eliot is out of favor—not "politically correct"—and so readers of all stripes miss out on the brilliant insight of the greatest poem of the past century, perhaps the greatest religious poem since *The Divine Comedy: Four Quartets*. Even fewer students, "general readers," and academics know such insightful and still-relevant older works as John Dryden's *Religio Laici or A Laymans Faith* (1682) and Alexander Pope's *An Essay on Man* (1734). I return to them here, along with

John Keats's sensuous and sensual poem "The Eve of St. Agnes," which embodies a "religion of love"; George Eliot's oft-abused novel *Adam Bede,* which followed upon her first book *Scenes from Clerical Life* and juxtaposes Anglicanism and Methodism, ritual and "fellow feeling"; James Joyce's great semi-autobiographical novel *A Portrait of the Artist as a Young Man* with its Romantic "hero" Stephen Dedalus, who opts not for the Roman priesthood but instead for a "priesthood of eternal imagination"; and Eliot's great essay-poem *Four Quartets,* the reading of which "bred" these thoughts here. I offer neither a history of the relation of literature and religion, although we proceed in a roughly chronological fashion, nor a systematic analysis of that relation, although I hope that my deliberately indirect manner of discussing these works yields some sustaining fruit. Still, as it happens, the texts I treat come from, and may to a degree represent, the three literary-historical periods from the Restoration through the mid-twentieth century. My chief concern is primarily with what these texts, old and more recent, can teach us about religious understanding that will allow us to live richer lives.

I am well aware that I treat only one form of religion here. Others exist, of course. But the writers whom I discuss in this book all think of religion *as* essentially Christianity, and so, although I by no means equate religion with Christianity, I sometimes fall into a habit encouraged by writers from Dryden to T.S. Eliot and beyond. At times, though, in any case, I write of *religious* matters, meaning issues that go beyond the sectarian, issues that Christianity treats from a position, acknowledged or not, as a part of the whole.

Literature works in, through, and by means of pattern. It is, said Ezra Pound, "language charged with meaning," poetry "language charged with meaning to the utmost possible degree."[2] I know of no better definitions. The (electrical) charges set off by imaginative writing, indeed defining it, require, as Pound also said, *condensare,* and he rightly cited Basil Bunting as a writer of extreme economy and precision (see Bunting's *Briggflatts,* for a notable example). Another helpful and valuable *aperçu* derives from the philosopher Jacques Maritain, as recently invoked by Archbishop of Canterbury Rowan Williams: art is a "made thing," and as such reflects the exigencies cited by Pound.[3] As a "made thing," art, of whatever kind, exists and functions by means of resonances and recurrences, prompting T.S. Eliot to write in *Ash-Wednesday* of the hope and the effort to "restor[e] / With a new verse the ancient rhyme," "rhyme" being another name for pattern.[4] His friend Ole Ez used the term "luminous detail,"[5] which, while not identical, of course, to "pattern," points to meaningful and significant matters that *stand out*. Repetition with difference creates this condition—and opportunity—for the reader. It also serves to distinguish imaginative and artful writing from mere exposition. Since pattern always involves at least a binary, *comparison* is, as Eliot averred, a key critical tool.

I am, also, of course, also well aware of the crucial contributions to literature made by "men of the cloth" over the centuries. To name but a select few establishes that importance: John Donne, George Herbert, Jonathan Swift, Gerard Manley Hopkins, Thomas Merton, R.S. Thomas, Paul Murray (all of whom, for what it is worth, of *a* Catholic persuasion). Study awaits of their contributions *as clergy*. Here, I can do little more than offer passing reference, largely for comparative purposes. I find R.S. Thomas particularly compelling, and it is very tempting to create room for his voluminous poems: a Welshman and Anglican priest, a dark and demanding, indeed exacting, figure. As I read this Kierkegaardian man, priest, and poet, I find a directness in his primal notion of God's (alleged) absence itself absent from, say, Eliot's understanding of Incarnation. Thomas, that is to say, writes, in the face of his own skepticism and doubt, from the position of the clergy, with their historical access to the mysteries unavailable to the ordinary layperson. He stands in need of no such mediation as we of the laity require; he *is*, after all, a mediator himself. As many readers acknowledge, directness also marks Thomas's poetic style and manner such that, perhaps oddly enough, doctrinal absence butts up against presence to the ideas versified. If I am right, Thomas would complicate matters unduly and no doubt prolong beyond reasonable parameters the study on which I am engaged, and so I will, with regret and apology, bracket him for the moment, at least.

The unabashedly didactic effort in which I am engaged here begins, then, as it must, with literature, the letter, the literal. That just so happens to be the subject of the chronologically first of my selected texts, Dryden's great but little-read essay-poem, which introduces the vital, indeed central notion of the *layman's faith,* an idea and a tradition long forgotten, although it includes such masterpieces as Sir Thomas Browne's *Religio Medici* as well as the very early Deistic effort of the brother of poet-priest George Herbert, Lord Herbert of Cherbury's *De religione laici.*[6] Published soon after the so-called Popish Plot, a little more than two decades into the Restoration of the Stuart regime following the beheading of Charles I in 1649 and the debacle of the Cromwellian or Puritan Interregnum, which one historian described as "the world turned upside down,"[7] *Religio Laici* defends Church and King but casts a much wider, moral, and theological apologia for the "via media." Dryden also confronts the "priesthood of all readers," locating in the Protestant revolution both the seeds and a striking and powerful symbol of sedition: one's way of reading, he dramatizes, establishes one's relation to authority, external or internal. Dryden also walks a thin and precarious tightrope between layistic individualism and assertion, on the one hand, and acceptance of outside authority, on the other. In short, Dryden's *Religio Laici* represents the essential lines that literature will take vis-à-vis religion over the next few centuries. It is important to recognize, as I have argued elsewhere, the lines linking the layman, the amateur, the "common reader," and the essayist, all of whom are interested in the essential questions of living as a human being in the world; uniting them is opposition to narrow, "professional," and academic interests.[8]

In confronting Deism, Dryden's essay-poem, one of the very first works to do so, signals the critical role exclusivism will play in Modern thinking. Deism famously posited a (unitarian) order in the universe, which it regarded as created by God and then left to man for his care; Deism thus bred, it seems, despite differences, such Modern thinking as Wordsworth's, Basil Bunting's, and Pound's: there *is* intelligence, and design, in the world, but there is no transcendent being operating upon it. Thus intones Dryden's Deist:

> ...the mighty Secret's found:
> *God* is that *Spring* of *Good*; *Supreme*, and *Best*;
> *We*, made to *serve*, and in that Service *blest*;
> If so, some *Rules* of Worship must be given,
> Distributed alike to all by Heaven:
> Else *God* were *partial*, and to *some* deny'd
> The Means his Justice shou'd for *all* provide. (43–49)[9]

But "Of all objections" to Christianity and its claim to Revealed Truth in Holy Scripture, writes Dryden in response, the "chief / To startle Reason, stagger frail Belief" (184–85) is the Deist's claim, "urge[d] anew" (168), that

> No *Supernatural Worship* can be *True*:
> Because a *general Law* is that alone
> Which must to *all*, and every *where* be known:
> A Style so large as not *this* Book can claim
> Nor ought that bears *reveal'd* Religions *Name*. (169–73)

Dryden puts very well the crucial argument for immanence (alone). Comparative religion is thus born as an idea, along with what Jacques Derrida referred to in another context as "seriality without paradigm."[10] Christianity lost its privileged position, which it has never recovered.

Dryden does still more in his *Religio Laici*. As he had done in his earlier, magisterial *Essay of Dramatick Poesy*, he *embodies* arguments and positions. The essay-poem proceeds, as that prose work did via characters, by means of imagined speakers, none of them fully realized, who enunciate the competing theological and ecclesiastical positions. Dryden works hard,

as a matter of fact, to make his readers understand choice as a
moral issue and a matter of character.

> Dar'st thou, poor Worm, offend *Infinity?*
> And must the Terms of Peace be given by *Thee?*
> Then *Thou* art *Justice* in the *last Appeal;*
> *Thy easie God* instructs Thee to *rebell:*
> And, like a King remote, and weak, must take
> What Satisfaction *Thou* art pleas'd to make. (93–98)

Representing truth as embodied is not the only way, though
it is very important, to which Dryden adheres in his *Religio
Laici* to Incarnational pattern, dramatizing it, in fact. By
insisting on truth as embodied, he reveals the fundamental
indirectness of that pattern. In like manner, Dryden emphasizes that God is approachable, not directly as the "Fanaticks"
suppose, but via the Scriptural text, which, he writes, "*speaks
it Self*" (368): God does not, in other words, speak to us
directly but, rather, through the letter, which must be read
(responsibly). The exordium that beautifully leads off the
poem emphasizes this very indirectness, along with the mediation that comes from instrumentality, setting the stage for
the crucial arguments to follow:

> DIM, as the borrow'd beams of Moon and Stars
> To *lonely, weary, wandring* Travellers,
> Is *Reason* to the *Soul:* And as on high,
> Those rowling Fires *discover* but the Sky
> Not light us *here;* So *Reason's* glimmering Ray
> Was lent, not to *assure* our *doubtfull* way,
> But *guide* us upward to a *better Day.*
> And as those nightly Tapers disappear
> When Day's bright Lord ascends our Hemisphere;
> So pale grows *Reason* at *Religions* sight;
> So *dyes,* and so *dissolves* in *Supernatural Light.* (1–11)

In *An Essay on Man*, Alexander Pope, often but wrongly
identified as Deistic, proceeds according to the Incarnational
pattern—while championing a fervent antisectarianism. Thus

Pope writes in resonant and key verses near the end of the fourth and final epistle:

> Slave to no sect, who takes no private road,
> But looks thro' Nature, up to Nature's God;
> Pursues that Chain which links th' immense design,
> Joins heav'n and earth, and mortal and divine.... (331–34)[11]

He soon follows with the poem's penultimate verse paragraph, which imaginatively dramatizes the pattern:

> God loves from Whole to Parts: but human soul
> Must rise from Individual to the Whole.
> Self-love but serves the virtuous mind to wake,
> As the small pebble stirs the peaceful lake;
> The centre mov'd, a circle strait succeeds,
> Another still, and still another spreads,
> Friend, parent, neighbour, first it will embrace,
> His country next, and next all human race,
> Wide and more wide, th' o'erflowings of the mind
> Take ev'ry creature in, of ev'ry kind;
> Earth smiles around, with boundless bounty blest,
> And Heav'n beholds its image in his breast. (361–72)

It perhaps seems a long way from Alexander Pope to John Keats, less than a century later. Maynard Mack has drawn the differences between the classical and Christian Pope and the pantheistic and Romantic William Wordsworth.[12] Keats, though, is not much like his fellow Romantic, preferring Dryden, as a matter of fact, at least toward the end of his young life, as seen in "Lamia." Whereas, Pope, of course, argues for "self-love" as the beginning of necessarily expanding love, Keats takes a definitely anti-Christian turn in his letters and in "The Eve of St. Agnes." In this great, oft-misunderstood poem, Keats pens a new *religion of love*, a desire of some standing, as attested by his great "Ode to Psyche."

It may seem further still from Keats to Cid Corman, who died in 2004, but the attempt to substitute for Christianity or to create a new religion, whether of love or something else, out of whole cloth—that is, one's own fertile fancy—knows few substantive differences. Although I do not plan to treat Corman in the pages that follow, I offer his voluminous—and seemingly off-the-cuff—poems as an instance, possibly extreme, of the direction lay writing on religion has been taking since the Reformation. I refer here specifically to "The Faith of Poetry" (1989), where Corman argues that "faith as 'fiction' merely tells us that any faith we abide by is and has to be of our own making/doing."[13] For us here, Corman will serve to complete the arc begun with Dryden: from a "layman's faith" to poetry's faith, Corman's verse and commentary suggestive of a primal, mystical, and talismanic power endemic to poetry, itself now gifted with agency.

In fact, Corman adduces one of his poems to just this effect in offering "The Faith of Poetry":

> ...it's time for
> something
> to happen and
> it is time,
> but nothing
> moves of itself;
> it must
> be moved...(1)[14]

Corman, who lived most of his later life in Japan and successfully translated haiku without knowing Japanese, proceeds to write, perhaps trying to clarify but waxing cryptic, in any case:

> Poetry then—as always—is religion. And if religion is anything—it is poetry. Unequivocally so. "In the beginning was the Word" (Logos—Memra). And poetry—as anyone knows who tastes of it—is the Word made flesh—as the prophets were, as Chuang-chou was, as Jesus and Gautama, as Tu Fu and Li Po, as Dante, as Shakespeare, as Blake, as Leopardi, as Hölderlin, as Kafka, and others were and—more to the point of us—are. (Ibid.)

Corman then quotes that "a man can receive nothing but what is given him," "he must increase, but I decrease," and "I am the bread of life," followed by this commentary:

> It isnt a church or a dogma, yet it recognizes how a structure can stand in and house faith; it recognizes the imperatives of community founded in the disciplines of an aware conjunction—meaning dance or song or music or any other work felt as work of the spirit—which the word "art" doesnt fully render. (Ibid.)[15]

After several poems, Corman moves to some kind of conclusion with these paragraphs, perhaps echoing George Oppen, who wrote: "I think there is no light in the world but the world / And I think there is light" (quoted as epigraph in Peter Gizzi, *The Outernationale*):[16]

> I say religion—not sect—not beholden to anyone but each of those who have drawn from and passed into word—Word. Pretentious? Only as all life is.
> An art of poverty—finding within the body of being enough—even more than enough—and finding in it too the breath's need to explain and explore itself as part of the air gone into it and coming forth. A kind of glory only poverty can yield—the bare all. With all the kinks of *nothing made flesh*.
> "Who will say this isnt love?"
> You are dead.
> Now speak.[17]

One has to wonder whether immanence could be carried further.

In response, at least to Corman, but to Keats as well, I will say this here, and attempt to develop the point and provide support of it as we go along: Love does not proceed directly from Being. In order to love, you have to, says Homer in *The Odyssey*, experience something like nothingness, undergo purgation, develop sympathy. Christian writers like Eliot, and, of course, Dante, emphasize a similar point. Understanding, with its implication of sympathy, mediates, making Love possible from Being. Sympathy is, to be sure, a female character, reflected in the Holy Mother Who gives birth to Jesus, without Whom we would likely not know Love as we do. The pattern is Incarnational and also Trinitarian:

Being	God
Understanding	Jesus Christ
Love	The Holy Spirit

To this pattern I would add another instance, given especially the writing of important figures like R.S. Thomas, Simone Weil, and Paul Murray (if not also Jacques Derrida): you perhaps begin with absence and move in, through, and by means of it to presence. For readers of literature, a writer's failure to acknowledge *embodied truth*—Gustave Flaubert comes to mind with his great (and seemingly bleak and devastating) novel *Madame Bovary*—need not land one in the throes of despair or hopelessness. Literature has a disillusioning and even purgatorial capacity. You, the reader, may need to complete the journey toward understanding.

I do not use the term "understanding" cavalierly. On the contrary, I wish modestly to suggest that literature asks for—indeed, demands—*understanding*. The point no doubt appears obvious, at least until we stop and observe. We do not—or no longer—talk much about "understanding" a poem, novel, or piece of nonfictional prose. Commonly, we talk of *reading* it, perhaps *interpreting* it, possibly of *analyzing* it—and worst of all, *dissecting* it. Understanding is more difficult, in part because not exclusive, in fact, more capacious.

    Understanding calls for and entails *participating in*. When we say "I understand," referring to a comment from another person, we mean not only that we have listened attentively, grasped the evident meaning of the words, and followed the line of thinking, but, also, that we "get" what that other person was "trying to get at." A certain sympathy is involved, willy-nilly. To an extent, and for the moment, we even "side" with that person and his or her saying, almost as if we inhabit that person's mind and heart—or perhaps he or she has momentarily flooded us. We "stand under" and see as she or he does. Thus we comprehend, we discern. There attends, as the dictionary reminds us further, "a state of cooperative or mutually tolerant relations." In short, to understand is "to perceive the meaning of; grasp the idea of," also "to be thoroughly familiar with; apprehend clearly the character, nature, or subtleties of," "to be conversant with" and "to assign a meaning to," further, "to grasp the significance, implications, or importance of"; finally, and intransitively, "to perceive what is meant; grasp the information intended to be conveyed." The street is two-way, between sender and receiver, and understanding suggests mutuality. As a noun, according to my Random House dictionary, understanding equals, first of all, "personal interpretation." (For an instance of understanding, participation in, and "personal interpretation," I suggest the wonderful essay on Gustave Flaubert's *Madame Bovary* by Andrew Lytle, the late Agrarian novelist, long-time editor of *The Sewanee Review*, and stalwart defender of Judeo-Christian traditions and values, included in his collection *The Hero with the Private Parts,* in the preface to which the critic writes brilliantly that "to read well you must write it down," which has led me to propose elsewhere a way of "writing-as-reading," a procedure that centrally involves "participation in."[18])

I want here to stress the relation between understanding and participation: in the first place, because it is necessary and, second, because understanding itself as an idea bears clear and critical Christian implications. The Incarnation itself instances God's participation in everyday, human existence; by taking on our form, our flesh, and in participating in "the world," He understands us. Odysseus had to visit the Kingdom of the Dead and to experience nothingness and death firsthand in order to develop the necessary capacities of giving, sympathizing, and controlling his reckless temper. The Jews, according to Cynthia Ozick, in the brilliant title essay of her collection *Metaphor and Memory,* founded morality upon the altar of mutuality and reciprocity, having learned through their own experience of enslavement "to envision the stranger's heart."[19] In Communion we participate, now, in the Body and Blood of Christ, coming to understand what *He* was, is, and did, and does, for us.

Furthermore, reading is the means of understanding, not an end in itself, as is so often implied these days. Understanding forms the end of reading—and Understanding plays, as I have suggested above, the central role between Being and Love. Literature becomes, accordingly, the means both of and to Understanding, and so of and to Christianity.

Finally, a word about the form of these chapters. Form matters, and the form I could hardly fail to choose is the essay: attempts, trials, necessarily marked by indirection. The essay is Incarnational form, or so I claim, and thus a certain rightness obtains between matter and form, which may turn out to be (very nearly) the same thing.

INTRODUCTION

"THE HINT HALF GUESSED, THE GIFT HALF UNDERSTOOD"

My parents, and especially my mother, always wanted, hoped, and half-expected that I would enter the Christian ministry, becoming a Baptist preacher. I never heard "the call," however, and wandered instead into the vocation of English professor. For years, I never felt complete, whole, or quite satisfied; all the while, I was writing about, and often teaching, religious aspects of the secular writings I embraced and professed. Revelation eventually came—though late—via a work of literature, T.S. Eliot's magisterial essay-poem *Four Quartets*—and in particular the single verse in *The Dry Salvages*: "The hint half guessed, the gift half understood, is Incarnation."[1]

Everything depends on the absence here of the expected definite article. I have come, accordingly, to believe with Eliot, to believe *incarnationally*, that the way to religious understanding proceeds in, through, and by means of (literary) texts and, therefore, that the pilgrim begins with literature (secular or sacred), does not stop there as we modernists and postmodernists are apt to think, but goes on, thanks to texts, to religion. I also agree with Old Possum, devout Anglo-Catholic: "the intelligent believer...finds the world to be so and so; he [or she] finds its character inexplicable by any non-religious theory: among religions he [or she] finds Christianity, and Catholic Christianity, to account most satisfactorily for the world and especially for the moral world within."[2] Disciplined observation leads to recognition of patterns, the paradigmatic of which is Incarnation (*plus* and *minus* the "the").

Most of my writings on religious topics were in the 1980s and early 1990s, at which point I may have appeared to detour into the essay. But, in fact, that venerable and protean form itself represents a telling and significant path toward understanding. It too seems like a detour, wandering about, rarely if ever proceeding in a strictly linear fashion, by indirections finding directions out (to invoke Shakespeare's old fool Polonius)—until, that is, one discovers there is *only* detour. My time with the essay, in other words, was hardly wasted, even from a religious standpoint. In fact, the essay in general has helped me much better to understand Incarnation and "incarnational art" (for despite Flannery O'Connor's dismissal of the very form in which she was at the time writing, the essay is, I have argued elsewhere, fundamentally Incarnational).[3] Steadfastly material, and rooted in the everyday and the particular, the essay opposes all forms of Gnosticism, if not also of such Manicheanism as O'Connor repudiates, the essay anti-spiritualistic at its very heart. While it may not be literature, or philosophy, but "almost" one and not quite the other (Eduardo Nicol),[4] the essay *is* or at least strives for artfulness and neither pretends to, nor I suspect can survive in, strictly religious, let alone dogmatic or doctrinal, air or terms. It fully embodies the indirectness that, I contend, marks the relation of literature and Christianity.

Rather than distinct and separate entities, independent and complete in and of themselves, literature and religion are each parts of a whole. Literature points toward, needs, finds its completion in religion; religion begins with texts and the reading of them—all of the great religions, historical and current, Western and Eastern alike, agree on this, at least. Unfortunately, it so often happens that a part usurps the structural position of the whole, dogmatically, even violently.

Literature traffics in bodies; it is thus, despite Flannery O'Connor's reduction, Incarnational. If it offers ideas, and it obviously does, they come (at least also) *embodied*: in persons, normally in situations familiar, that we recognize as (more or less) realistic. Novels of ideas exist, of course: Hermann Hesse's *Siddhartha* springs immediately to my mind. That book—which I am inclined to denominate as an essay, along with, say, George Eliot's *Adam Bede*—does confront ideas but not exactly directly, for there is always the mediation of person, Siddhartha himself, Vasudeva, and others. The mediation of the body is always present. Literature is not, in other words, philosophy or theology. The latter are direct in the way that literature is mediated. To be sure, borderline cases exist, for instance, Thomas Carlyle's *Sartor Resartus*, but they are relatively rare and tend to confirm the point.

Works of literature—fiction and nonfiction alike, in verse as well as prose—quite often, unlike essays, show us how *not to* live. They are, in other words, not only dramatic but also negative "agents of disillusionment," as Herbert N. Schneidau has finely put it (*Sacred Discontent: The Bible and Western Tradition*).[5] Literature works to disabuse us of certain ideas as it seeks to redirect, if not to refine, our feelings. Often, of course, literature does what William Wordsworth famously proposed in ushering in Romanticism: it expands our capacity for sympathy and human and social engagement, enlarging the understanding, all the while. (William J. Harvey long ago showed how George Eliot, for one, so constructs and structures her fiction as to allow, if not persuade, her reader to do just that.[6]) Another thing literature does, as Pound urged, is that it directs us to live in the present, rather than pine over the past or whore after the future, "the vanity of human wishes" a perennial theme, the drama of "great expectations" another. A tension—a relation—thus develops between hope and enlightenment.

The *present moment* matters—Pound's emphatic "NOW." In *Four Quartets*, Eliot labors heroically to recast human attention on Incarnation's revelation: it is not just the "luminous" moment or "the moment in the rose garden" or a Wordsworthian "spot of time" that looms with meaning, perhaps available on and to reflection, which itself carries considerable danger. Given the

Incarnation, timelessness "intersects" time *at every moment,* each instant burning with meaning.

I can think of no better illustration of these central points than Robert Browning's well-known dramatic monologue "Fra Lippo Lippi," Incarnational art both represented and—according to the current jargon—*theorized.* The speaker is, of course, the lusty, sensuous, and sensual Renaissance painter escaped for the nonce from his sequestered quarters at the de Medici villa and confronted by a sentry as a vibrant parade of revelers passes nearby. (In contrast, see G.K. Chesterton's beautiful essay "A Piece of Chalk,"[7] which, surprisingly enough, given the author's proclaimed orthodoxy, depicts the merely transcendent position that Fra Lippo Lippi opposes in his Prior.) Thus the Prior, as represented by the Friar, is disparaging realism—and the literal—as he surveys the artwork:

> How? What's here?
> Quite from the mark of painting, bless us all!
> Faces, arms, legs and bodies like the true
> As much as pea and pea! it's devil game!
> Your business is not to catch men with show,
> With homage to the perishable clay,
> But lift them over it, ignore it all,
> Make them forget there's such a thing as flesh.
> Your business is to paint the souls of men—
> Man's soul, and it's a fire, smoke...no, it's not...
> It's vapor done up like a newborn babe—
> (In that shape when you die it leaves your mouth)
> It's...well, what matters talking, it's the soul!
> Give us no more of body than shows soul!
> Here's Giotto, with his Saint a-praising God,
> That sets us praising—why not stop with him?
> Why put all thoughts of praise out of our head
> With wonder at lines, colors, and what not?
> Paint the soul, never mind the legs and arms!
> Rub all out, try at it a second time....(175–94)[8]

Fra Lippo Lippi's response—not to his Prior, of course, but to the sentry with his hand around his throat—is decisively

Incarnational (even) in his fallen-ness and (even) as he wanders off at the end with a seeming encomium on beauty alone:

> Now, is this sense, I ask?
> A fine way to paint soul, by painting body
> So ill, the eye can't stop there, must go further
> And can't fare worse! Thus, yellow does for white
> When what you put for yellow's simply black,
> And any sort of meaning looks intense
> When all beside itself means and looks naught.
> Why can't a painter lift each foot in turn,
> Left foot and right foot, go a double step,
> Make his flesh liker and his soul more like,
> Both in their order? Take the prettiest face,
> The Prior's niece... patron-saint—is it so pretty
> You can't discover if it means hope, fear,
> Sorrow or joy? won't beauty go with these?
> Suppose I've made her eyes all right and blue,
> Can't I take breath and try to add life's flash,
> And then add soul and heighten them threefold?
> Or say there's beauty with no soul at all—
> (I never saw it—put the case the same—)
> If you get simple beauty and naught else,
> You get about the best thing God invents:
> That's somewhat: and you'll find the soul you have missed,
> Within yourself, when you return him thanks. (198–220)

The Prior here no doubt speaks for many Christians, a formidable caricature of partial—that is, *half*—understanding. (It is precisely the souls [of cows] that Chesterton claims to paint, never mind that no one has seen one or can define it, unable to get down the "things" before him, and evidently unaware of his heterodoxy in bypassing immanence for transcendence, nothing less than a forgery in its directness.) A critical Incarnational point is precisely "Both in their order," "each foot *in turn*" (italics added). As the Friar says later in the poem, "God made it all" (285). What, then, is "it all about? / To be passed over, despised? Or dwelt upon, / Wondered at?" (290–92). Nowhere is the Friar more suggestive, or appealing, than in his incisive observation that "This world's no blot for us, / Nor blank; it means intensely, and means good: / To find its meaning is my meat and drink" (313–15)—an apt statement for an Incarnational artist.

Eliot's friend Ezra Pound—"*il miglior fabbro*," said he, dedicating *The Waste Land* to Ole Ez—wrote somewhere of "Swift perception of relations, hallmark of genius." That is to say, "the cluster of associations triggered by" "The apparition of these faces in the crowd; / Petals on a wet, black bough" ("In a Station of the Metro")—"Odysseus' descent into Hades, Dante's visit to the Inferno, Persephone and Demeter—is present in the twentieth-century subway, but only for those who can see."[9] "*Perception of relations*" and "swift perception of relations": relations are *there*—that is, *here*—to be perceived. They exist, independently of the perceiver, the observer—although they depend upon his or her perception to be activated. By "relations," Pound clearly means, among many other things, Odysseus and us, Confucius and us, Mencius and us, Jefferson and us, and light and understanding, history and order (or meaning). Pound believed, in other words, in what he described as " 'the intelligence working in nature and requiring no particular theories to keep it alive.' "[10] According to Cookson, "His dislike of monotheistic religion is part of the...struggle against intolerance, monopoly and uniformity. 'The glory of the polytheistic anschauung is that it never asserted a single and obligatory path for everyone.' "[11]

Eliot appears to echo Pound, but hardly to identify with him, when, in *Four Quartets* especially, he speaks of "the pattern" that humankind everywhere seeks, perhaps the key to the mysteries that men and women have always intuited but could only "half" understand, Manicheans at the core. Indeed, Eliot identifies the nature of the (merely physical) world *as it is,* that necessary first step that he describes so evocatively in his essay on Blaise Pascal, which I cited above from *Selected Essays.* Having treated the literal and the familiar, Eliot moves—allegorically for us here—to that necessary, critical, and crucial other "dimension." The way is difficult to understand, although simple. Eliot was no saint, and neither are we, of course, but I doubt very much that he would be writing, and writing so precisely, if he was not convinced that he could help us by *elucidating* (the central aim, he said, of criticism). Here is response to Pound's immanentism—as well as his asseverations against the arbitrary and the monolithic, for by speaking of Incarnation (*minus* the "the") Eliot identifies that pattern the paradigmatic instance of which is *the* Incarnation, thereby establishing that this structure is and (always) has been everywhere present, available, and apparent (to those with eyes to see). The importance of this point can hardly be overestimated. Eliot implicitly confronts not just Pound but also other important immanentists like Wordsworth, Basil Bunting, and Cid Corman, all religious poets who eschew Christianity in favor of some power, force, or intelligence alive and working in the universe. Eliot's—and Christianity's—Incarnational pattern is just such a living presence. Unlike such other writers, Eliot brings transcendence to immanence, for *the* Incarnation is God's becoming man, thereby enfleshing the pattern available to all men and women everywhere but so often missed, gotten half-right.

Here as well lies an answer to Jacques Derrida and his notions of *differance* and the "trace," for Eliot too insists on *relation*, thereby "deconstructing" simple either/or and neither/nor. Binary oppositions reveal a trace of the other that effectively crumples their claim to essential and identifying difference. The critical relations partake of the pattern defined by both Incarnation and the Trinity.

Our job as *readers* of texts graphic and otherwise is to recognize and apprehend relations—*swiftly* (just as Pound teaches, so as to forestall the eruptions, presumptions, and egoism of reflection). We must recognize the exact (nature of the) relation between God and man, spirit and flesh, fact and fiction—and thus literature and religion, and more particularly, Christianity. What work—or vocation—is more important?

Eliot variously identified the capacity—the capaciousness—of which I speak (incidentally, in ways echoing the later and somewhat different ideas of both F. Scott Fitzgerald, in "The Crack-Up," and James Baldwin, in "Notes of a Native Son," who write, respectively, "the test of a first-rate intelligence is the ability to hold two opposed ideas in the mind at the same time, and still retain the ability to function" and "one would have to hold in the mind forever two ideas which seemed to be in opposition)."[12] In "The Metaphysical Poets," cutting to the heart of modern malaise (and incapacity), Eliot says that a "poet's mind" when "properly equipped for its work"

> is constantly amalgamating disparate experience; the ordinary man's experience is chaotic, irregular, fragmentary. The latter falls in love, or reads Spinoza, and these experiences have nothing to do with each other, or with the noise of the typewriter or the smell of cooking; in the mind of the poet these experiences are always forming new wholes.[13]

The passage is key, the ideas seminal. In another essay written around the same time, and perhaps taking a cue from Alexander Pope's *An Essay on Criticism*, Eliot defines wit as precisely this capaciousness, which he locates in Andrew Marvell:

> ...wit is not erudition; it is sometimes stifled by erudition, as in much of Milton. It is not cynicism, though it has a kind of toughness which may be confused with cynicism by the tender-minded. It is confused with erudition because it belongs to an educated mind, rich in generations of experience; and it is confused with cynicism because it implies a constant inspection and criticism of experience. It involves, probably, a recognition, implicit in the expression of every experience, of other kinds of experience which are possible....[14]

"Wit" so defined as capaciousness appears to depend upon, if not derive from, that skill or technique that Eliot identifies, along with "analysis," as "the tools of the critic": *comparison*.[15] In his most famous and influential essay "Tradition and the Individual Talent," Eliot confirms the relation, embracing "a judgment, a comparison, in which two things are measured by each other."[16]

"Both/and" prevails, we may say, invoking Derrida, although the point revolves around the relation, established by comparison and apprehended by "wit," that is, the perceiving mind able to connect and to make "wholes" out of "the chaotic, irregular, [and] the fragmentary." The result appears to be the wonderful union symbolized in the moving and powerful evocation of Elizabethan times in *East Coker*, second of *Four Quartets*. The passage is rife with meaning and significance, anticipating as it does the closing rendition of words artful and potent as "The complete consort dancing together" (*Little Gidding*):

> The association of man and woman
> In daunsinge, signifying matrimonie—
> A dignified and commodious sacrament.
> Two and two, necessarye coniunction,
> Holding eche other by the hand or the arm
> Which betokeneth concorde.

"Necessarye coniunction" names the point exactly.

Eliot himself figures the issue. Already in *The Sacred Wood* (1920), several years before he "converted" to Anglo-Catholicism, joining the Church of England, he embodies the Incarnational pattern without, apparently, being aware of it. Thus he writes, for instance, "Romanticism is a short cut to the strangeness without the reality, and it leads its disciples only back upon themselves."[17] More tellingly, beginning to treat the relation between literature and matters outside it, notably "ideas," Eliot observes: "The temptation, to any man who is interested in ideas and primarily in literature, to put literature into the corner until he has cleared up the whole country first, is almost irresistible."[18] In this regard, he faults Matthew Arnold, who, for instance, like the aforementioned Romantics, jumps directly to the structural equivalent of God, avoiding the necessary "detour." We can all, if honest, I think, attest to the power of the temptation to move outside *literary* to cultural criticism of one sort or another, including that of religion. In "Religion and Literature" (1935), Eliot completes the thought begun in *The Sacred Wood*: there he had sought to show that the critic, and by implication any reader, begins by *comparing and analyzing* works of literature; now he adds that the critic must not stop with the purely literary effort.

Indeed, he opens "Religion and Literature" with this unusually straightforward and direct assertion: "What I have to say is largely in support of the following proposition...: Literary criticism should be completed by criticism from a definite ethical and theological standpoint."[19] His own critical commentary follows this arc with great fidelity—as attested by a comparison of *The Sacred Wood* and *Homage to John Dryden* (1924) with *For Lancelot Andrewes* (1928), *After Strange Gods* (1933), *Essays Ancient and Modern* (1935), *The Idea of a Christian Society* (1940), and *Notes Towards the Definition of Culture* (1948).

Matthew Arnold famously predicted in the Victorian period the imminent replacement of religion by poetry; not long thereafter, Stephen Dedalus, James Joyce's semi-autobiographical protagonist in *A Portrait of the Artist as a Young Man* (1916) rejected the Roman Catholic priesthood in favor of art, declaring himself a "priest of eternal imagination";[20] both Arnold and Joyce (at least) share long-standing desires perhaps traceable to the "layman's faith" tradition of the seventeenth century and, beyond that, Martin Luther's defining Protestant idea of "the priesthood of all believers." Writing in 1682, and engaging both the traditions, John Dryden offered a brilliant essay-poem on the priesthood of all readers: *Religio Laici or A Laymans Faith.* Dryden, Arnold, and Joyce are but three important writers engaging issues of moment and lasting concern. Protestantism figures prominently in the debates concerning the relation of literature and Christianity, but the issue is by no means either anti- or a-Roman.

In spite of the significant number of major literary figures who were "Divines"—for example, John Donne, George Herbert, Jonathan Swift, Laurence Sterne, R.S. Thomas, all of these Anglican, incidentally—literature has always been largely a *lay* effort. Certainly poems and novels alike represent the interests of a more or less amateurish readership, to whom they are most often directed. I suspect "the common reader," an analogue of the laity (as of the amateur and also the essayist, or so I have argued elsewhere), and a notion adumbrated by Dr. Johnson in the eighteenth century and resuscitated by

Virginia Woolf early in the twentieth century, is more important in the history and evolution of literature than modern-
day critics like to acknowledge.

That literature *shows* its relation to religion is a major argument in and of the essays that comprise this book. The "pilgrim's progress," that is to say, the journey of the "intelligent
believer"—to take once more Eliot's term and notion—begins
with—but does not end with—texts, sacred as well as secular,
of course. It is the secular with which I concern myself here,
although, to make enquiry manageable without reducing the
issue or the evidence, I concentrate on literary texts with overt
religious interests, concerns, and direction. Ultimately, or so I
would contend, *all literary texts* to more or less degree are
Incarnational, their essential structure partaking of and participating either positively or negatively in the pattern that makes
of everything, at every moment, everywhere, revelatory and
meaningful.

In treating literature and religion and their relation, it is difficult to ignore or minimize the importance and the position of
Ezra Pound. Despite the efforts of critics and scholars like the
late William Cookson and Herbert N. Schneidau, his pro-
foundly religious understanding is largely dismissed, in favor
of tiresome discussion of his admittedly alien and poorly and
dangerously conceived politics. Too little light is brought to
bear on Pound's religious thinking, and too few recognize the
light emanating from his religious views, however strange they
may initially appear. Of considerable importance is Pound's
insistence on immanence, alongside resistance to all forms of
transcendence.

Also principally concerned with "the thing," we ought to
remember, were Marianne Moore and William Carlos
Williams—and Martin Heidegger; do not forget such appo-
site efforts as Rudolf Bultmann's to "demythologize" Holy
Scripture. But in a footnote, Eliot once averred that "the
spirit killeth, but the letter giveth life,"[21] and C.H. Sisson
lately has insisted on the *literal* Resurrection.[22] Pound, in any
case, makes religious implications unmistakable, and so allows

us to see with perhaps unparalleled clarity and power the issues at stake. My interest here lies neither in dismissing Pound nor in elevating him.

His sense of immanence is particularly attractive, I think, in part because it derives from an apparent exotic nature, evoking the unfamiliar and smacking somewhat of the forbidden and even the dangerous. Pound, it is clear, does not go beyond the literal—whereas Christianity goes *by way of* the literal, which it never leaves behind, on to "another dimension." In so doing, the bread—of the sacrament of Communion, for example—does not "stand for" something else but, rather, *participates in it.*

As to the relation of literature and religion, Pound left no such essay as Eliot did. He did, though, in "The Wisdom of Poetry," offer extended and valuable remarks on the relation:

> As the poet was, in ages of faith, the founder and emendor of all religions, so, in ages of doubt, is he the final agnostic; that which the philosopher presents as truth, the poet presents as that which appears as truth to a certain sort of mind under certain conditions.
>
> "To thine own self be true...." were nothing were it not spoken by Polonius, who has never called his soul his own.
>
> The poet is consistently agnostic in this; that he does not postulate his ignorance as a positive thing. Thus his observations rest as the enduring data of philosophy. He grinds an axe for no dogma. Now that mechanical science has realised his ancient dreams of flight and sejunct communication, he is the advance guard of the psychologist on the watch for new emotions, new vibrations sensible to faculties as yet ill understood. As Dante writes of the sunlight coming through the clouds from a hidden source and illuminating part of a field, long before the painters had depicted such effects of light and shade, so are later watchers on the alert for colour perceptions of a subtler sort, neither affirming them to be "astral" or "spiritual" nor denying the formulae of theosophy. The traditional methods are not antiquated, nor are poets necessarily the atavisms which they seem. Thus poets may be retained as friends of this religion of doubt, but the poet's true and lasting relation to literature and life is that of the abstract mathematician

to science and life. As the little world of abstract mathematicians is set a-quiver by some young Frenchman's deductions on the functions of imaginary values—worthless to applied science of the day—so is the smaller world of serious poets set a-quiver by some new subtlety of cadence.

At any rate, "For the initiated the signs are a door into eternity and into the boundless ether."[23]

For Pound, then, it is clear, religion may be experienced through literature. Essentially, in fact, religion is *in* literature for the immanentist poet. For Eliot, differently, the Christian poet, religion represents the completion of literature, the City of God toward which the work of literature directs the reader, leading him or her to religion in, through, and by means of itself. For Pound, authority is individual; he remained very much an American, and a Westerner (he was born in Idaho), something of an independent and "free spirit." There is as well about him an accompanying sense of the layman engaged in offering *his own, individual faith*. In these senses, he looks within—whereas Eliot turns outside the self, toward the Church. Pound misses the whole, in other words, getting only half the "story" of Incarnation, "the hint *half* guessed, the gift *half* understood." The whole consists of *both* immanence *and* transcendence.

And yet—*Four Quartets*, on which I draw so heavily, may very well strain orthodoxy. Like my undergraduate teacher Vincent E. Miller,[24] I suspect Eliot's greatest poem of some heterodoxy, although I have very little interest in settling the issue (even if I could). I have alluded above to a certain positive relation among the essayist, the amateur, the "common reader," and the "layman's faith," and have claimed that *Four Quartets* is an essay-poem. As an essayist, I further contend, Eliot also bears some of the marks of the layperson, which he, of course, was. Why, after all, would he have written what he has unless he thought that this secular, possibly heterodox work—an instance of "tradition" *and* individualism, which, after all, he signaled as an inseparable relation in his single most important essay—could be helpful to "the intelligent believer" on the path of understanding? Like Pope in *An Essay on Man*, furthermore, he seems to avoid mention of Christ, and he pointedly refers to "Incarnation," not *the* Incarnation. In the allegorical lyric constituting the important fourth section of *East Coker*, Eliot evidently refers to the Church as "the dying nurse," opening wide the path of speculation.

Students sometimes allege that my class discussion turns into a sermon, and I reckon there is truth to the charge. I make no apologies, however, here or there, for literature derives its power from both form and significance, and significance has to do with meaning for oneself: the text is never walled-off from the outside world, self-contained, or irrelevant.

Teaching is itself, moreover, inseparable from (a kind of) preaching, and the kind of ministry that I perform and practice is not limited by the sort of "professionalism" that posits the professor as unrelated to her or his students. There is, I have come to realize, thanks in part to the role of "pastoral counselor" I played during 18 years as the department's graduate director, a pastoral function in teaching, all too rarely accepted. "Both/and"s rise up to greet and embrace sometimes in the most unlikely of places. One of them is (the relation of) student and teacher, another literature and religion.

1

Essaying the *Via Media*:
John Dryden's *Religio Laici* and
Alexander Pope's *An Essay on Man*

Dryden's great verse epistle, his 1682 defense of Church and King, *Religio Laici or A Laymans Faith,* and Pope's theodicy *An Essay on Man,* published in four epistles in 1734, are both, in fact, essays. As such, they embody a certain individualism. Many claimed at the time, and many more subsequently, that Pope had proved himself a Deist, an argument that drew support from his earlier "Universal Prayer" and the use of his friend and Deist Henry St. John, Viscount Bolingbroke, as addressee in *An Essay on Man.* Dryden took on "the Deist" in his Anglican apologia, among the first to do so, while writing as a self-described and proclaimed layman. He earned praise for so doing from personalities such as Thomas Creech, translator of Lucretius: in one of three commendatory poems, all similar in tone, texture, and focus, added to the 1683 edition of the poem, Creech wrote, "'Tis nobly done, a Layman's Creed profest, / When all our Faith of late hung on a Priest; / His doubtfull words like Oracles receiv'd, / And when we could not understand, believ'd."[1]

A profound anticlericalism marks Dryden's poem, as it does so much of his work, both before and after his conversion to the Church of Rome, within four or five years of his "layman's faith" (e.g., *Absalom and Achitophel,* perhaps his greatest work, opens, "In pious times, e'r Priest-craft did begin...").[2] A Roman Catholic all his life, despite the entailed hardships and the ministrations of such prominent Anglican friends as Bishop

Francis Atterbury and Jonathan Swift, Pope was far less fla-grant in his asseverations against the clergy, although as an "Erasmian Catholic," he could pen such verses as those in *An Essay on Criticism* praising "that *great, injur'd* Name, / (The *Glory* of the Priesthood, and the *Shame*!)" and condemning "*Holy Vandals*" (693–94, 696).[3]

As a "layman's faith," Dryden's essay-poem belongs in a little-known seventeenth-century tradition of efforts on behalf of the laity. The tradition had some important texts, though limited in volume, including Lord Herbert of Cherbury's *De religione laici* and, the most famous, Sir Thomas Browne's *Religio Medici*.[4] Without calling attention to the fact, *An Essay on Man* forms part of the effort to represent a nonclerical, nonprofessional, amateur's take on religion that focuses, not unlike Deism itself, on matters crucial to everyone's salvation. As Dryden puts it, after rejecting Papist authoritarianism, and making clear the direction of his religious thinking ("*God wou'd not leave Mankind without a way*" [296; Dryden's ital-ics]), "If *others* in the *same Glass better* see / 'Tis for *Themselves* they look, but not for *me*: / For *MY* Salvation must its Doom receive / Not from what *Others*, but what *I* believe" (301–4). After all, Dryden concludes, "The things we *must* believe, are *few*, and *plain*" (432).

Both *An Essay on Man* and *Religio Laici or A Laymans Faith* are essays in part because of their "essentialist" and lay posi-tions; by the same token, you could say that they belong to the layman's faith tradition because of their basic essayistic texture. Elsewhere, at some length, I have argued that, while not inter-changeable exactly or synonymous, the terms "essayist," "lay-man," "amateur," and—a fourth term important especially to Dryden's text—"common reader" are analogues one of anoth-er.[5] Essay complements "layman's faith" and makes the natural, and expected, form for the latter, as in *Religio Medici*. A long and important tradition of essays in verse extends through the seventeenth and into the eighteenth century, of course.

What I have not treated before is the relation between Deism, on the one hand, and this essay–layman's faith attitude and texture. Certainly a positive relation exists between the essay and Anglicanism, its existence and function, variously exemplified, as the *via media* between Roman Catholicism and (extreme) Protestantism. The essay too is a *via media* creature, whose truths *emerge* rather than are asserted, a point and a fact borne out in Dryden's *Religio Laici.*

I shall not repeat arguments I have made elsewhere regarding Dryden's essay-poem.[6] Here, then, I emphasize how Dryden works to address the situation of laymen, post-Reformation. Evidently, reared as an Anabaptist (biographical evidence regarding Dryden before the Restoration is slight), and from his earliest work flamingly anticlerical, he writes in his "layman's faith" of the Reformation that "This good had full as bad a Consequence" (399). The line itself reflects perfectly the tension that marks *Religio Laici.*

After treating, and answering, the Deist's "objections" to revealed religion, the Bible, and "Supernatural Worship," an answer to the charge that *part-iality* indicts and invalidates Judeo-Christian thinking, about all of which more directly, Dryden turns to the Catholic and his claims on behalf of the *universality* of that Church.

Tension here too is apparent and important. Dryden begins by writing of the reading that "bred" his own efforts in his "layman's faith": a heavy, scholarly tome, done by a Roman Catholic priest, Father Richard Simon (and now translated as *The Critical History of the Old Testament* by the poet's young friend Henry Dickinson, to whom, in fact, this section of the poem is addressed) and—*mirabile dictu*—admitting and exposing errors in the text on which the Roman Church bases its claim to supreme and ultimate authority. Anticlericalism striates the passage, Dryden now free as a layman, thanks to the Reformation, to think, and write, according to his own conscience, a "good" with "full as bad a Consequence," it turns out. Alongside this freedom appear responsibility and restraint donning the form of modesty and humility:

> Thus far my Charity this path has try'd;
> (A much unskilfull, but well meaning guide:)
> Yet what they are, ev'n these crude thoughts were bred

> By reading that, which better thou hast read,
> Thy Matchless Author's work: which thou, my Friend,
> By well translating better dost commend:
> Those youthfull hours which, of thy Equals most
> In *Toys* have *squander'd*, or in *Vice* have *lost*,
> Those hours hast thou to Nobler use employ'd;
> And the severe Delights of Truth enjoy'd.
> Witness this weighty Book, in which appears
> The crabbed Toil of many thoughtfull years,
> Spent by thy Authour, in the Sifting Care
> Of *Rabbins* old Sophisticated Ware
> From Gold Divine; which he who can well sort
> May afterwards make *Algebra* a Sport.
> A Treasure, which if *Country-Curates* buy,
> They *Junius*, and *Tremellius* may defy:
> Save pains in various readings, and Translations;
> And without *Hebrew* make most learn'd quotations. (224–43)

The digs appear gratuitous, though relatively mild, smacking of ubiquitous pre-Reformation anticlericalism; still, the texture of these verses reflects less of "faith" and more of the "layman." At any rate, proceeding, Dryden writes:

> A Work so full with various Learning fraught,
> So nicely pondred, yet so strongly wrought,
> As Natures height and Arts last hand requir'd:
> As much as Man cou'd compass, uninspir'd:
> Where we may see what *Errours* have been made
> Both in the *Copiers* and *Translaters Trade*:
> How *Jewish*, *Popish*, Interests have prevail'd,
> And where *Infallibility* has fail'd. (244–51)

Although at first glance this passage may seem largely digressive, or even gratuitous, closer examination reveals a critical connection with Dryden's principal themes. A book is, after all, at the center of the argument, and reading he ties unmistakably to the Reformation: the Lutheran "priesthood of all believers" becomes, in Dryden's hands here, the *priesthood of all readers*. Reading, in fact, becomes the site where tension is played out, where, indeed, one's relation to God appears vividly. Dryden draws out all these implications brilliantly and effectively, as well as efficiently.

In the next verse paragraph, Dryden begins to examine the "Popish" position on the sacred text, its preservation, and the validity of claims to authority of both transmission and interpretation. He starts by neatly tying in an anticlerical surmise with the monumental issues that he will proceed to unfold:

> For some, who have his secret meaning ghes'd,
> Have found our Authour not too *much a Priest*:
> For *Fashion-sake* he seems to have recourse
> To *Pope*, and *Councils*, and *Traditions* force:
> But he that *old* Traditions cou'd subdue,
> Cou'd not but find the weakness of the *New*:
> If *Scripture*, though deriv'd from *heav'nly birth*,
> Has been but carelessly preserv'd on *Earth*;
> If *God*'s *own People*, who of *God* before
> Knew what we know, and had been promis'd more,
> In fuller Terms, of Heaven's assisting Care,
> And who did neither *Time*, nor *Study* spare
> To keep this Book *untainted, unperplext*;
> Let in gross *Errours* to corrupt the *Text*:
> Omitted *paragraphs*, embroyl'd the *Sense*;
> With vain *Traditions* stopt the gaping Fence,
> Which every common hand pull'd up with ease:
> What Safety from such *brushwood-helps* as these?
> If *written words* from time are not secur'd,
> How can we think have *oral Sounds* endur'd?
> *Immortal Lyes* on *Ages* are intail'd:
> And that some such have been, is prov'd too plain;
> If we consider *Interest, Church*, and *Gain*. (252–75)

Dryden gives a strong and full argument, pulling no punches, it seems. Reading this passage, we will likely conclude that Scripture is incomplete—*partial*. The argument here is directed toward Church—and especially priestly—perfidy, rather than to Scriptural fallibility.

As the poem's side-note specifically says, the issue of the following verse paragraph concerns "*the Infallibility of Tradition, in General.*" Dryden here imagines an unnamed Popish interlocutor, as he had earlier with "the Deist"; his argument continues now those begun in the previous lines regarding the greater problems posed to inclusiveness and *im*-partiality by the oral emphasis of Roman Catholicism (as opposed to Protestantism's privileging of the written):

> Oh but says one, *Tradition* set aside,
> Where can we hope for an *unerring Guid*?
> For since th' *original* Scripture has been lost,
> *All* Copies *disagreeing, maim'd* the *most*,
> Or *Christian Faith* can have no *certain* ground,
> Or *Truth* in *Church Tradition* must be found. (276–81)

In developing the argument in the next verse paragraph, Dryden lets his thesis *emerge* from countering the antithesis; that thesis—ultimate reliance on God and God alone—has already been suggested and will now figure prominently in the poem, clear through to the end—the first couplet is rhetorically brilliant, introducing new arguments that build carefully upon groundwork already laid:

> Such an *Omniscient* Church we wish indeed;
> 'Twere worth *Both Testaments*, and cast in the *Creed*:
> But if *this Mother* be a *Guid* so sure,
> As can all *doubts resolve*, all *truth secure*,
> Then her *Infallibility*, as well
> Where Copies are *corrupt*, or *lame*, can tell;
> Restore *lost Canon* with as little pains,
> As *truly explicate* what still *remains*:
> Which yet no *Council* dare *pretend* to doe;
> Unless like *Esdras*, they cou'd *write* it new:
> Strange Confidence, still to *interpret* true,
> Yet not be sure that all they have explain'd,
> Is in the blest *Original* contain'd. (282–94)

Dryden will shortly develop the telling argument against interpreting in general, but here he establishes the dependence of interpretation upon sound and sure scholarship, the point building upon his earlier panegyric on the allegedly unpriestly

Father Simon's pioneering *Critical History of the Old Testament*. In proceeding, Dryden sounds the layman's note of modesty, safety, and reasonableness, an implicit invocation of and reliance upon a *via media* and an unmistakable pledge and demonstration of *faith*:

> More Safe, and much more modest 'tis, to say
> *God wou'd not leave Mankind without a way*:
> And that the *Scriptures*, though not *every where*
> Free from Corruption, or intire, or clear,
> Are uncorrupt, sufficient, clear, intire,
> In *all* things which our needfull *Faith* require.
> If *others* in the *same Glass better* see
> 'Tis for *Themselves* they look, but not for *me*:
> For *MY* Salvation must its Doom receive
> Not from what *OTHERS*, but what *I* believe. (296–304)

Moral tone, introduced early (especially 93–98), becomes critical at this point, and Dryden effects a balanced perspective, both even-handed in the treatment of opposing and opposed views and moderate in intellection. The side-note reads: "*Objection in behalf of Tradition; urg'd by Father* Simon," which is actually a subtle reflection of the same kind of balance.

> Must *all Tradition* then be set aside?
> This to affirm were Ignorance, or Pride.
> Are there not many points, some needfull sure
> To saving Faith, that Scripture leaves obscure?
> Which every Sect will wrest a several way
> (For what *one* Sect Interprets, *all* Sects *may*.)
> We hold, and say we prove from Scripture plain,
> That *Christ* is *GOD*; the bold *Socinian*
> From the *same* Scripture urges he's but *MAN*.
> Now what Appeal can end th' important Suit;
> *Both* parts *talk* loudly, but the *Rule* is *mute*? (305–15)

The argument returns us squarely to the critical and central matter of *part*-iality, itself based in reason and carefully

connected now, via the reference to Socinus, to the unorth-
dox and in fact Deistical. Moreover, Dryden locates the crux
of faith and belief in the Incarnation. He skillfully skirts
this plagued question, however, and rather than offer an
opinion, opts to focus on what appears to be a larger—but
is actually a narrower—question. He falls back, clearly, on
an appeal to a structure built into the moral frame of the
universe, like *Incarnation*, thus voiding the question of *the*
Incarnation. This is the *layman's faith*—nonsectarian, modest, balanced, based in reasonableness: let there be no mistake, however; unlike Deists, Dryden does not deny *the*
Incarnation.

> Shall I speak plain, and in a Nation free
> Assume an honest *Layman's Liberty*?
> I think (according to my little Skill,
> To my own Mother-Church submitting still:)
> That many have been sav'd, and many may,
> Who never heard this Question brought in play.
> Th' *unletter'd* Christian, who believes in *gross*,
> Plods on to *Heaven*; and ne'er is at a loss:
> For the *Streight-gate* wou'd be made *streighter* yet,
> Were *none* admitted there but men of *Wit*. (316–25)

Dryden here modulates into a sharp focus on issues of reading
and the layman's nonprofessional interests and needs:

> The few, by Nature form'd, with Learning fraught,
> Born to instruct, as others to be taught,
> Must Study well the Sacred Page; and see
> Which Doctrine, this, or that, does best agree
> With the whole Tenour of the Work Divine:
> And plainlyest points to Heaven's reveal'd Design:
> *Which* Exposition flows from *genuine Sense*;
> And which is *forc'd* by *Wit* and *Eloquence*. (326–33)

In the remainder of this long verse paragraph, Dryden argues
for the primacy of the Church Fathers and *"first Traditions"*
(342), which, however, because flawed, constitute "not *Truth*

but *Probability*" (345). His own faith is that "Truth by its own Sinews will prevail" (349).

Now comes the Papists' second objection, which affords Dryden the opportunity to focus squarely upon the matter of the part and the whole, a variation, that is, of the Deist's earlier argument, and a refutation of Rome's claims of catholicity:

> The partial *Papists* wou'd infer from hence
> *Their* Church, in last resort, shou'd Judge the *Sense*.
> But first they wou'd assume, with wondrous Art,
> *Themselves* to be the *whole*, who are but *part*
> Of that vast Frame, the Church; yet grant they were
> The handers down, can they from thence infer
> A right t' interpret? or wou'd they alone
> Who brought the Present, claim it for their own? (356–63)

From this question, Dryden proceeds to his single clearest thesis-statement in the essay-poem, a reasoned, balanced, and modest assertion of lay rights and responsibilities based in and deriving from a reliance on God Himself as Ultimate Authority: not Church nor the individual's "inner light" or "private reason." Of course, God comes mediated; we know Him only through the Scripture. Dryden thus walks a fine line, performing a delicate and precarious balancing act, indeed.

> The *Book*'s a *Common Largess* to *Mankind*;
> Not more for *them*, than *every* Man design'd:
> The *welcome News* is in the *Letter* found;
> The *Carrier*'s not Commission'd to *expound*.
> It *speaks* it *Self*, and what it does contain,
> In all things *needfull* to be *known*, is *plain*. (364–69)

Effectively, Dryden borrows the Deist argument, substituting for their Book of Nature that of Holy Scripture: the latter, he claims, is as clear *to everyone* (wherever it matters to the layperson) as Nature herself.

Now, he is free to lambaste the clergy—and will include both Protestant preachers and Popish priests in his sweeping condemnations. Priests were exclusive, partial, and self-serving *before* the Reformation, and "new presbyter" has proved to be, as the familiar saying went, but "old priest writ large." The anticlericalism in the following verse paragraph is severe, but Dryden saves his harshest, most brutal remarks for the followers of the "private spirit." First, then, the Papists, who insisted on "expounding" what, given its clarity, stands in no more need of interpretation than the everyday things seen in nature:

> In times o'ergrown with Rust and Ignorance,
> A gainfull Trade their Clergy did advance:
> When want of Learning kept the *Laymen* low,
> And none but *Priests* were *Authoriz'd* to *know*:
> When what small Knowledge was, in them did dwell;
> And he a *God* who cou'd but *Reade* or *Spell*;
> Then *Mother Church* did mightily prevail:
> She parcel'd out the Bible by *retail*:
> But still *expounded* what She *sold* or *gave*;
> To keep it in *her Power* to *Damn* and *Save*:
> *Scripture* was *scarce*, and as the Market went,
> Poor *Laymen* took *Salvation* on *Content*;
> As needy men take Money, good or bad:
> *God*'s Word they had not, but the *Priests* they had.
> Yet, whate'er *false Conveyances* they made,
> The *Lawyer* still was *certain* to be paid.
> In those dark times they learn'd their knack so well,
> That by long use they grew *Infallible*:
> At last, a knowing Age began t' enquire
> If *they* the *Book*, or *That* did *them* inspire:
> And, making narrower search, they found, thô late,
> That what they thought the *Priest*'s, was *Their* Estate:
> Taught by the *Will produc'd*, (the written Word)
> How long they had been *cheated* on *Record*.
> Then, every man who saw the Title fair,
> Claim'd a Child's part, and put in for a Share:
> Consulted Soberly his private good;
> And sav'd himself as cheap as e'er he cou'd. (370–97)

The Reformation was inevitable, justified, necessary.

And yet—"This good had full as bad a Consequence" (399): an admission that laymen, freed, acted irresponsibly; given license, they became licentious, lacking, precisely, in those qualities and virtues on which Dryden has insisted—and embodied: reasonableness, balance, moderation, restraint, and modesty. Dryden's indignation rises to the level of *saevo*, and his language, particularly the diction, descends to a level not seen before in this poem, and in fact rare in his poetry. This becomes satire of the Juvenalian sort, in a poem otherwise professedly Horatian:

> The Book thus put in every vulgar hand,
> Which each presum'd he best cou'd understand,
> The *Common Rule* was made the *common Prey*;
> And at the mercy of the *Rabble* lay.
> The tender Page with horney Fists was gaul'd;
> And he was gifted most that loudest baul'd:
> The *Spirit* gave the *Doctoral Degree*:
> And every member of a *Company*
> Was of *his Trade*, and of the *Bible free*.
> Plain *Truths* enough for needfull *use* they found;
> But men wou'd still be itching to *expound*:
> Each was ambitious of th' obscurest place,
> No measure ta'n from *Knowledge*, all from *GRACE*.
> (400–412)

The situation, and the behavior, is, in fact, opposite that embodied in the Catholic Father Richard Simon, a fact available to solicited comparison.

> *Study* and *Pains* were now no more their Care;
> *Texts* were explain'd by *Fasting*, and by *Prayer*:
> This was the Fruit the *private Spirit* brought;
> Occasion'd by *great Zeal*, and *little Thought*.
> While Crouds unlearn'd, with rude Devotion warm,
> About the Sacred Viands buz and swarm,
> The *Fly-blown Text* creates a *crawling Brood*;
> And turns to *Maggots* what was meant for *Food*.
> *A thousand daily Sects rise up, and dye*;
> *A Thousand more the perish'd Race supply*.
> So all we make of Heavens discover'd Will
> Is, not to have it, or to use it ill.

> The Danger's much the same; on several Shelves
> If *others* wreck *us*, or *we* wreck our *selves*. (413–26)

With what no doubt strikes us as more daring than it did his contemporary readers, Dryden equates sects with insects, reducing them as far as imaginable.

Religio Laici or A Laymans Faith now confirms its basic essay nature, revealing itself as virtually the paradigmatic instance of the form. The verses just preceding, especially 423–26, establish unmistakably the moral nature of Dryden's concern, and the immediately succeeding lines pick up on that and advance it as they echo points already firmly established. Moreover, and importantly, Dryden has not heretofore argued *for* the Church of England, that *via media* that John Henry Newman famously characterized as known best in its differences. He could have derived the point straight from this essay-poem, for Dryden has allowed, as already mentioned, the positive simply to *emerge*—as alternative: "What then remains, but, waving each Extreme, / The Tides of Ignorance, and Pride to stem? / Neither so rich a Treasure to forgo; / Nor proudly seek beyond our pow'r to know" (427–30).

At this point, Dryden returns to the tightrope already positioned. He has contended that the layman need be concerned only about a few, major points, and those, he says, are clearly stated in the Scripture. "Since," however, and with a pun or two, "men *will* believe more than they *need*; / And every man will make *himself* a Creed: / In doubtfull questions 'tis the safest way / To learn what unsuspected Ancients say," for, after all, " 'tis not likely *we* shou'd higher Soar / In search of Heav'n, than *all the Church before*" (433–38). And if, we find, the Scripture and the Church Fathers disagree, what then? Dryden again states his basic position, adding a nuance or two that fully embodies tension and the struggle for balance and moderation:

> 'Tis some Relief, that points not clearly known,
> Without much hazard may be let alone:
> And, after hearing what our Church can say,

If still our Reason runs another way,
That private Reason 'tis more Just to curb,
Than by Disputes the publick Peace disturb.
For points obscure are of small use to learn:
But *Common quiet* is *Mankind's concern*. (443–50)

The responsible layman should thus willingly "consult" his Church on controverted and questionable matters—the *Established* Church—and then, being committed to reason, if She runs afoul of reason, (again willingly) curb the private *in favor of the common good*—thus sacrificing the part that is the self to the whole. It is a powerful declaration of a *via media*.

Dryden next adds three couplets, which a great many readers regard as throw-away lines, wishing he had stopped just above. I think, on the contrary, that Dryden was wise to include them, a striking contrast with the brilliant imagery of the poem's exordium. The lines not only point to the essayistic nature of the effort here, but also reiterate Dryden's fundamental commitment to the clarity and the ubiquity of "*Sacred Truth*," which, he insists, and concludes, shines through any representation of it:

Thus have I made my own Opinions clear:
Yet neither Praise expect, nor Censure fear:
And this unpolish'd, rugged Verse, I chose;
As fittest for Discourse, and nearest Prose:
For, while from *Sacred Truth* I do not swerve,
Tom Sternhold's, or *Tom Shadwell's Rhimes* will serve. (451–56)

The justly praised exordium, with its masterful images of sun, moon, and reason, establishes Dryden's own submission to Revelation. Reason, he says in the first of the essay-poem's braced and thematically telling triplets, serves us as instrument, and medium: "So *Reason's* glimmering Ray / Was lent, not to *assure* our *doubtfull* way, / But *guide* us upward to a *better Day*" (5–7), an incisive description of his own purposive movement in his "layman's faith." Dryden makes sure we understand: "When Day's bright Lord ascends our Hemisphere; / So pale grows *Reason* at *Religions* sight; / So *dyes*, and so *dissolves* in *Supernatural Light*" (9–11).

In this opening verse paragraph, Dryden turns to the age-old and universal quest for "*one first principle*" (14), a pattern and a center, the "Summum Bonum." That having proved elusory, despite the continuing and laborious efforts, he considers the Deist and the threat posed by this belief that "*finite Reason* [can] reach *Infinity*" (40). The Deist, writes Dryden, thinks himself on firmer ground in locating the secret in God, "that *Spring* of *Good*; *Supreme*, and *Best*" (44). Dryden then describes the essential Deist argument concerning parts and whole:

> *We*, made to *serve*, and in that Service *blest*;
> If so, some *Rules* of Worship must be given,
> Distributed alike to all by Heaven:
> Else *God* were *partial*, and to *some* deny'd
> The Means his Justice shou'd for *all* provide. (45–49)

Dryden never explicitly rejects this critical argument, swerving instead, beginning the guiding effort throughout to turn theological and (later) ecclesiological positions into moral and ethical choices:

> Thus Man by his own strength to Heaven wou'd soar:
> And wou'd not be Oblig'd to God for more.
> Vain, wretched Creature, how art thou misled
> To think thy Wit these God-like Notions bred!
> These Truths are not the product of thy Mind,
> But dropt from Heaven, and of a Nobler kind. (62–67)

The Deist does not acknowledge that his reason has been enabled by Revelation, his insight merely like "the borrow'd beams of Moon and Stars" (1):

> *Reveal'd Religion* first inform'd thy Sight,
> And *Reason* saw not, till *Faith* sprung the Light.
> Hence all thy *Natural Worship* takes the *source*:
> 'Tis *Revelation* what thou thinkst *Discourse*.
> Else, how com'st *Thou* to see these truths so clear,
> Which so obscure to *Heathens* did appear? (68–73)

Even Plato, Aristotle, Plutarch, Seneca, and Cicero—"Those Gyant Wits, in happyer Ages born" (80)—"no such Piles cou'd raise / Of *Natural Worship*, built on *Pray'r* and *Praise*, / To *One sole God*" (82–84). How, then, dare the modern Deist: "Dar'st thou, poor Worm, offend *Infinity*?" (93). Dryden's reiterated (positive) point is simple and straightforward: "A *Mulct thy* Poverty cou'd never pay / Had not *Eternal Wisedom* found the way" (103–4). Therefore, "Look humbly upward, see his Will disclose" (101). Dryden's argument speeds ahead, declaring, among other things, the Deist foiled.

> For granting we have Sin'd, and that th' offence
> Of *Man*, is made against *Omnipotence*,
> Some Price, that bears *proportion*, must be paid;
> And *Infinite* with *Infinite* be weigh'd.
> See then the *Deist lost: Remorse* for *Vice*,
> *Not* paid, or *paid*, *inadequate* in price:
> What farther means can *Reason* now direct,
> Or what Relief from *humane Wit* expect?
> *That* shews us *sick*; and sadly are we sure
> *Still* to be *Sick*, till *Heav'n* reveal the *Cure*:
> If then *Heaven*'s *Will* must needs be understood,
> (Which must, if we want *Cure*, and *Heaven*, be *Good*)
> Let all Records of *Will reveal'd* be shown;
> With *Scripture*, all in equal ballance thrown,
> And *our one Sacred Book* will be *That one*. (111–25)

The final appeal, and pledge, is to "Heaven," and Heaven's "Will" as revealed in Holy Scripture, to which position reason leads Dryden. In spite of all, tension appears, and prominently here.

This same texture appears in the following verse paragraph, Dryden arguing not so much the truth of Scripture as its superiority. The lines acquire perhaps unanticipated and therefore surprising importance.

> *Proof* needs not here, for whether we compare
> That Impious, Idle, Superstitious Ware
> Of *Rites, Lustrations, Offerings*, (which before,

In various Ages, various Countries bore)
With *Christian Faith* and *Vertues*, we shall find
None answ'ring the great ends of humane kind
But *This one Rule of Life: That* shews us best
How *God* may be *appeas'd*, and *Mortals blest*. (126–33)

As he pursues this argument, Dryden states that what human-kind needs was *first found in the soul*; it would later appear in "the Book." God, in other words, made known to us the essentials of salvation *before Christ*, an analogue of pattern preceding the Incarnation.

Whether from length of *Time* its worth we draw,
The *World* is scarce more *Ancient* than the *Law*:
Heav'ns early Care prescrib'd for every Age;
First, in the *Soul*, and after, in the *Page*.
Or, whether more abstractly we look,
Or on the *Writers* or the *written Book*,
Whence, but from *Heav'n*, cou'd men unskill'd in Arts,
In several Ages born, in several parts,
Weave such *agreeing Truths*? or *how*, or *why*
Shou'd *all* conspire to cheat us with a *Lye*?
Unask'd their *Pains*, *ungratefull* their *Advice*,
Starving their *Gain*, and *Martyrdom* their *Price*. (134–45)

"The Book" itself, argues Dryden, proves its own validity, for "what is *Taught* agrees with *Natures Laws*" (151), a telling point, indeed.

Nature, from now on, becomes somewhat problematical, for Dryden begins to build on his earlier asseverations against the Deist, and no doubt others, whose "*easie God* instructs Thee to *rebell*" (96). Christianity is distinguished, says Dryden, precisely by means of its difference from and opposition to human nature (and easiness—he evidently has in mind so-called Latitudinarians):

All Faiths *beside*, or did by *Arms* ascend;
Or *Sense* indulg'd has made *Mankind* their *Friend*:
This *onely* Doctrine does our *Lusts* oppose:
Unfed by Natures Soil, in which it grows;
Cross to our *Interests*, curbing Sense, and Sin;

Oppress'd without, and undermin'd within,
It thrives through pain; its own Tormentours tires;
And with a stubborn patience still aspires.
To what can *Reason* such Effects assign
Transcending *Nature*, but to *Laws Divine*?
Which in that Sacred Volume are contain'd;
Sufficient, clear, and for that use ordain'd. (156–67)

While clearly "the Soil" in which Christian doctrine grows, nature is, just as clearly, (to be) refined, if not transcended.

Now follows the Deist's objection to these arguments, in many ways the crux of the lay position as Dryden represents it in his *Religio Laici*—the issue of universality, real catholicity, parts/whole all over again, now represented in terms of *confining*:

But stay: the *Deist* here will urge anew,
No *Supernatural Worship* can be *True*:
Because a *general Law* is that alone
Which must to *all*, and every *where* be known:
A Style so large as not *this Book* can claim
Nor ought that bears *reveal'd* Religions *Name*.
'Tis said the sound of a *Messiah*'s *Birth*
Is gone through all the habitable Earth:
But still that Text must be confin'd alone
To what was *Then* inhabited, and known:
And what Provision cou'd from *thence* accrue
To *Indian* Souls, and Worlds discover'd *New*?
In other parts it helps, that Ages past,
The Scriptures there were *known*, and were *imbrac'd*,
Till Sin spread once again the Shades of Night:
What's that to these who never *saw* the Light? (168–83)

Dryden's answer seems genuine, straightforward—rather than venture a direct argument, he appeals once more to God, who surely did not "confine" His pity, sympathy, and love, but somehow effected a way for those B.C. to be saved:

Of all Objections this indeed is chief
To startle Reason, stagger frail Belief:
We grant, 'tis true, that Heav'n from humane Sense

Has hid the secret paths of *Providence*:
But *boundless Wisedom, boundless Mercy*, may
Find ev'n for those *be-wildred* Souls, a *way*:
If from his *Nature Foes* may Pity claim,
Much more may *Strangers* who ne'er heard his *Name*.
And though *no Name* be for *Salvation* known,
But that of his *Eternal Sons* alone;
Who knows how far transcending Goodness can
Extend the *Merits* of *that Son* to *Man*?
Who knows what *Reasons* may his *Mercy* lead;
Or *Ignorance invincible* may plead? (184–97)

Christ Jesus *is* the Way, but one should be wary of "confining" that way: Eliot shows how *the* Incarnation is the paradigmatic instance of Incarnation, a structure and a pattern everywhere and at all times available, albeit not often recognized, necessitating God taking on human flesh to establish once and for all the Way.

At this point, Dryden acknowledges that his sense of "charity" leads him to the above hope and faith, along with past testimony that nature—with its observable patterns—*may* have been sufficient before God became man in the Person of Jesus (after all, Dryden has said that "the *Law*" was inscribed "First, in the *Soul*, and after, in the *Page*"):

Not onely *Charity* bids hope the *best*,
But *more* the great Apostle has exprest:
That, if the Gentiles, (whom no Law inspir'd,)
By Nature did what was by *Law requir'd*;
They, who the written Rule had never known,
Were to themselves both Rule and Law alone:
To Natures plain indictment they shall plead;
And, by their Conscience, be condemn'd or freed.
Most righteous Doom! because a *Rule reveal'd*
Is *none* to *Those*, from whom it was *conceal'd*.
Then those who follow'd *Reasons* Dictates right;
Liv'd up, and lifted high their *Natural Light*;
With *Socrates* may see their Maker's Face,
While Thousand *Rubrick-Martyrs* want a place. (198–211)

For whatever reason or reasons, Dryden adds a verse paragraph unusual in nature for this essay-poem. It is by no means
digressive, although it may appear gratuitous. These six couplets admit—they do not respond to the Deist, or anyone else,
for that matter—that the charitable arguments he has advanced
do not jibe with St. Athanasius's widely respected views. The
paragraph seems oddly important, certainly establishing the
issue as a crux for the poet.

> Nor does it baulk my *Charity*, to find
> Th' *Egyptian* Bishop of another mind:
> 'Tis hard for *Man* to doom to *endless pains*
> All who believ'd not all, his Zeal requir'd;
> Unless he first cou'd prove he was inspir'd.
> Then let us either think he meant to say
> *This Faith*, where *publish'd*, was the onely way;
> Or else conclude that, *Arius* to confute,
> The good old Man, too eager in dispute,
> Flew high; and as his *Christian* Fury rose
> Damn'd all for *Hereticks* who durst *oppose*. (212–23)

Confronting in his "layman's faith" an opponent—the Deist—
reminiscent of Arius, Dryden responds differently, *containing*
his own "*Christian* Fury." The verse paragraph establishes
something else, at least—or it confirms it—and that is the
speaker's charitableness, for he professes to think the best of
Athanasius, embodying, in other words, the very virtue he
praises.

Such sympathy, and charity, as Dryden here and elsewhere
reveals, and embodies, is, of course, characteristic of "layman's
faiths." Although they are not necessarily Latitudinarian—
Dryden's certainly is not—a definite tenderness toward
humankind marks them. A strict interpretation would put it
that they are already "contaminated" by the (modern) feelings
that they might well otherwise reject and repudiate.

Written when he was no more than 21 (and perhaps as young
as 17), *An Essay on Criticism* is brilliantly conceived and just

as brilliantly executed. By means of the comparative and contrasting terms "wit" and "judgment," Pope pens a poem that is criticism, criticism that is a poem. He calls the effort an "essay," and rightly so. His *trial*, also an *assay*-ing, succeeds because Pope was (already) a masterful artist, refusing to separate judgment from wit absolutely, poetry from the essay, criticism from creation. As Aubrey Williams pointed out a half-century ago, in refusing especially to separate wit and judgment, Pope aligned himself with the Ancients, against Peter Ramus, Hobbes, and Locke, helping to preserve poetry as something more than mere dress or decoration.[7] Pope had wisdom well beyond his years, perhaps a greater mind than that of Dryden, although a smaller heart. He knew that criticism is, at bottom, "*Gen'rous Converse*" (641), or it is nothing, and that in the critic we should never allow "the man" to "be lost" (523), nor criticism lose its moral basis—else all is lost. He also knew the critical importance, therein, of relating *part* to part and *part* to *whole*—he made the age-old problem the heart of *An Essay on Criticism*.[8] It figures thereafter in almost everything he wrote.

Instances of anticlericalism mark *An Essay on Criticism*, as I observed above. "The *Monks*," Pope said, "finish'd what the *Goths* begun" (692), ensuring the Dark Ages. He adds, referring to the heroic figure for whom he felt, as a fellow Catholic, so much empathy: "At length, *Erasmus*, that *great, injur'd* Name, / (The *Glory* of the Priesthood, and the *Shame!*) / *Stemm'd* the *wild Torrent* of a *barb'rous Age*, / And drove those *Holy Vandals* off the Stage" (693–96). Closer to his own time, writes Pope, evidently referring to William and Mary, "The following License of a Foreign Reign / Did all the Dregs of bold *Socinus* drain; / Then Unbelieving Priests reform'd the Nation, / And taught more *Pleasant* Mrethods of Salvation" (544–47). Pope's politics thus echoes Dryden's, and his basic religious sensibility seems, at the very least, compatible with the past master's.

Dryden, of course, writes directly and forthrightly as a layman, and although the terms are analogues one of another, Pope is the professed essayist. Both poets write as essayists and laymen, and they both, as it happens, treat issues of reading, which they see as critical to their contemporary cultural situations, religious and political. (As I have said, the "common reader" is, along with "amateur," another analogue of layman and essayist.) Pope, I think, learned from writing *An Essay on Criticism*, from what he discovered in writing there about reading, and he goes on to apply those lessons in his later cultural commentary.

One of the most important of these lessons, I argue, has to do with parts/whole, the matter central to the work of reading and of critical commentary. As I have shown in an article published in 1979 ("Poetic Strategies in *An Essay on Criticism*, Lines 201–559"), the perennial problem serves not only as focus of the essay-poem's second (of three) sections, but also becomes the structural basis of that section. Pope treats the various parts that critics grow fond of, lean upon, and wrongfully equate with the whole, including language, imagery, and rhyme, as well as preference, for instance, of Ancients or Moderns, one's "own *Side*, or *Mind*" (452): "Thus Criticks, of less *Judgment* than *Caprice*, / *Curious*, not *Knowing*, not *exact*, but *nice*, / Form *short ideas*; and offend in *Arts* / (As most in *Manners*) by a *Love to Parts*" (285–88). Further, "Most Criticks, fond of some subservient Art, / Still make the *Whole* depend upon a *Part*, / They talk of *Principles*, but Notions prize, / And All to one lov'd Folly Sacrifice" (263–66). The issue is, clearly, a moral one—and in *Dunciad* IV, at the end of his life, Pope directly satirizes just this reduction that he claims ends in "Self." In *An Essay on Criticism*, the ideal is *impartiality*, fully represented in the image of the ideal critic (who bears, unfortunately or not, resemblance to the poet himself as he represents himself throughout)—every word here tells:

> But where's the Man, who Counsel *can* bestow,
> Still *pleas'd* to *teach*, and yet not *proud* to *know*?
> Unbiass'd, or by *Favour* or by *Spite*;
> Not *dully prepossest*, nor *blindly right*;
> Tho' Learn'd, well-bred; and tho' well-bred, sincere;

> Modestly bold, and Humanly severe?
> Who to a *Friend* his Faults can freely show,
> And gladly praise the Merit of a *Foe*?
> Blest with a *Taste* exact, yet unconfin'd;
> A *Knowledge* both of *Books* and *Humankind*;
> *Gen'rous Converse*; a *Soul* exempt from *Pride*;
> And *Love to Praise*, with *Reason* on his Side? (631–42)

The following lines epitomize Pope's critical position in *An Essay on Criticism* as they point the direction his subsequent cultural criticism will take, figured in determined opposition to *part*-iality, and its analogue sectarianism, with which he contrasts a complex capacity for both/and thinking:

> Some *foreign* Writers, some our *own* despise;
> The *Ancients* only, or the *Moderns* prize:
> (Thus *Wit*, like *Faith*, by each Man is apply'd
> To *one small Sect*, and All are *damn'd beside*.)
> Meanly they seek the Blessing to confine,
> And force *that Sun* but on a *Part* to Shine.... (394–99)

I cannot but read "*Sun*" as also "Son."

Not surprisingly, a significant lack of agreement appears between Dryden and Pope on the matter of doctrinal (and ecclesiastical) differences and their importance to the person Eliot calls the "intelligent believer." Sectarian differences weigh heavily in *Religio Laici or A Laymans Faith*, and Dryden, staking a claim, appears to participate. In Pope, any position smacking of sectarianism is a critical problem. The question is large, and must be faced at some point: can you go straight to the religious and theological substance, transcending or effecting a bypass of doctrine, dogma, and other ecclesiastical concerns? For Dryden, the answer is no; those concerns—of the surface or "dress," some might say—*embody* the (substantive) issues.

Well-known verses in *An Essay on Criticism* at least touch on the entailed issues. I refer to the following:

> Poets like Painters...unskill'd to trace
> The *naked Nature* and the *living Grace*,
> With *Gold* and *Jewels* cover ev'ry Part,

And hide with *Ornaments* their *Want of Art*.
True Wit is *Nature* to Advantage drest,
What oft was *Thought*, but ne'er so well *Exprest*.
. . . .
But true *Expression*, like th' unchanging *Sun*,
Clears, and *improves* whate'er it shines upon,
It *gilds* all Objects, but it *alters* none.
Expression is the *Dress* of *Thought*. . . . (293–98, 315–18)

We may well choose to quarrel with the poet here: not only is
there "clearing" and "improvement," but does not that "gild-
ing" affect, *alter*, and change? In any case, the passage complicates too-easy opposition of inside/outside, substance and
dress or ornament, the "real" and the putatively superficial.
Suppose, furthermore, that "expression" is already *inside*
(which would be consonant with the poem's earlier notion—
lines 82–83—that wit, rather than judgment, "manages" wit).
The problem, that is to say, may lie with us, accustomed as
we—now—are to conceive of dress as the merely outer, ines-
sential, and decorative. Eliot once averred that whereas the
"spirit killeth," "the letter giveth life."[9]

We stand on firmer ground in returning to Pope's central
concern with parts/whole. The early poem "The Universal
Prayer"—sometimes labelled the Deist's prayer (and omitted,
perhaps for that reason, from Aubrey Williams's popular
Riverside Edition) is about nothing else. Apparently written in
1715, almost 20 years before *An Essay on Man*, with which it
was once thought to be a companion piece, it cuts to the very
heart of Pope's interest and his abiding positions. The opening
stanza is a ringing endorsement of universalism:

Father of All! in every Age,
    In every Clime ador'd,
By Saint, by Savage, and by Sage,
    Jehovah, Jove, or Lord![10]

In fact, Pope pointedly extends God's available blessings without confinement:

Yet not to Earth's contracted Span,
    Thy Goodness let me bound;

> Or think Thee Lord alone of Man,
>> When thousand Worlds are round. (21–24)

Allegiance to "the whole" Pope now embodies in equally pointed antisectarianism:

> Let not this weak, unknowing hand
>> Presume Thy Bolts to throw,
> And deal Damnation round the land,
>> On each I judge thy Foe. (25–28)

Pope also prays for salvation from "foolish Pride" (32) and for a certain capaciousness, in line with but also beyond *An Essay on Criticism*:

> Teach me to feel another's Woe;
>> To hide the Fault I see;
> That Mercy I to others show,
>> That Mercy show to me. (37–40)

The last stanza returns us to the poem's beginning, reiterating the universality of the Deity being invoked and praised:

> To Thee, whose Temple is all Space,
>> Whose Altar, Earth, Sea, Skies;
> One Chorus let all Being raise!
>> All Nature's Incense rise! (49–52)

"The Universal Prayer" thus rings the changes on true Catholicity.

It is little wonder, then, that Pope would describe himself, in his theodicy, as "Slave to no sect" (4.330). In an Anglican country, with Anglican Divines among his best friends, the Roman Catholic Alexander Pope might well assume such a position, especially since he suffered for his Church (forbidden to attend university, to live within 10 miles of London, and so forth).

An Essay on Man is a great, although much-maligned, poem. It tells the story of order in the universe, the inversion of which is the later, four-part *Dunciad*. Designed, writes Pope, to "vindicate the ways of God to Man" (1.16)—John Milton said *Paradise Lost* would "justify the ways of God to man"—this essay-poem shows how "Parts relate to whole" (3.21), "plastic Nature" at work (3.9). The parts/whole relation contributes to effective *tension*, not unity, nor absolute difference: for instance, "jarring int'rests of themselves create / Th'according music of a well-mixed State" (3.293–94). Pope also sounds the notes and strikes the poses by now familiar to us from having considered, albeit briefly, some of his earlier work:

> For Forms of Government let fools contest;
> Whate'er is best administer'd is best:
> For Modes of Faith, let graceless zealots fight;
> His can't be wrong whose life is in the right.
> In Faith and Hope the world will disagree,
> But all Mankind's concern is Charity:
> All must be false that thwart this One great End,
> And all of God, that bless Mankind or mend.
>   Man, like the gen'rous vine, supported lives;
> The strength he gains is from th' embrace he gives.
> On their own Axis as the Planets run,
> Yet make at once their circle round the Sun:
> So two consistent motions act the Soul;
> And one regards Itself, and one the Whole. (3.303–16)

Near the end of *An Essay on Man*, Pope distinguishes God's way of loving from man's: "God loves from Whole to Parts: but human soul / Must rise from Individual to the Whole" (4.361–62), starting, in fact, from love of self. The point is of crucial importance because it suggests, unmistakably, the pattern called Incarnation: the structure is always that of "inferior" to "superior," thus *indirect* and *mediated*. Pope has already driven the point home:

> Slave to no sect, who takes no private road,
> But looks thro' Nature, up to Nature's God;
> Pursues that Chain which links th' immense design,
> Joins heav'n and earth, and mortal and divine... (4.330–34)

Nature is thus means, not end.

Whereas *An Essay on Man* represents love as ever-expanding, *The Dunciad* pictures the triumph of Dulness and the return of "Chaos and old Night" as reduction, narrowing, and confinement. Lost is the capacity for seeing and effecting—for understanding—relation, as revealed in the victory of mere professionalism:

> The critic Eye, that microscope of Wit,
> Sees hairs and pores, examines bit by bit:
> How parts relate to parts, or they to whole,
> The body's harmony, the beaming soul,
> Are things which Kuster, Burman, Wasse shall see,
> When Man's whole frame is obvious to a *Flea*. (4.233–38)

A key passage near poem's end picks up and weaves into a clear text(ile) the various threads we have been tracing, making the pattern clear. The first speaker is Dulness herself, the second a favored minion, a clergyman evidently of the Deistical sort (perhaps Samuel Clarke):

> "O! would the Sons of Men once think their Eyes
> And Reason giv'n them but to study *Flies*!
> See Nature in some partial narrow shape,
> And let the Author of the Whole escape:
> Learn but to trifle; or, who most observe,
> To wonder at their Maker, not to serve."
> "Be that my task (replies a gloomy Clerk,
> Sworn foe to Myst'ry, yet divinely dark;
> Whose pious hope aspires to see the day
> When Moral Evidence shall quite decay,
> And damns implicit faith, and holy lies,
> Prompt to impose, and to dogmatize:)
> Let others creep by timid steps, and slow,
> On plain Experience lay foundations low,
> By common sense to common knowledge bred,
> And last, to Nature's Cause thro' Nature led.
> All-seeing in thy mists, we want no guide,
> Mother of Arrogance, and Source of Pride!
> We nobly take the high Priori Road,
> And reason downward, till we doubt of God:

Make Nature still incroach upon his plan;
And shove him off as far as e'er we can:
Thrust some Mechanic Cause into his place;
Or bind in Matter, or diffuse in Space.
Or, at one bound o'er-leaping all his laws,
Make God Man's Image, Man the final Cause,
Find Virtue local, all Relation scorn,
See all in *Self*, and but for self be born:
Of nought so certain as our *Reason* still,
Of nought so doubtful as of *Soul* and *Will.*
Oh hide the God still more! and make us see
Such as Lucretius drew, a God like Thee:
Wrapt up in Self, a God without a Thought,
Regardless of our merit or default." (4.453–86)

A devastating—and relevant—critique, devastatingly clear. Few if any contribute more importantly to Dulness's triumph, the obliteration of Light, and the return of Darkness than the clergy: in fact, "*Religion* blushing veils her sacred fires" (4.649). Not even poetry can save the Day. Nature has, before, become end, and would-be pilgrims seek no "guide." Discarnation replaces the Incarnational pattern.

Two quite different interpretations and understanding of faith, Dryden's *Religio Laici* and Pope's *An Essay on Man*. Some of these differences may be attributable to the former's writing as a member of the Established Church, the latter a member of the Church of Rome—within a few short years Dryden would, of course, convert to Roman Catholicism and pen an apologia for his new Church, the quite different poem *The Hind and the Panther* (in which few if any vestiges remain of the essay or the essayistic). Dryden's essay-poem works so brilliantly in part because he is able to represent the Church of England *as* the "middle way." As he paints, and embodies, that position, Anglicanism fulfills the needs, expectations, and demands of the ordinary layman. I think it an open question whether, dramatically, the determinative factor is Anglicanism or the layman's faith. In any case, the act itself of speaking *as a layman* suggests that *any* religious positions acceptable to the layman must meet—whether or not conform to—certain conditions of *his* choosing. The layman may, in the end, following Dryden's embodied lead, submit to the "Mother Church," but tension remains, and the layman is well on his way toward broad and inclusive demands and expectations. Pope instances a rather mediated continuation of the layman's faiths.

2

"A grander scheme of salvation than the chryst\<e\>ain religion": John Keats, a New Religion of Love, and the Hoodwinking of "The Eve of St. Agnes"

John Keats was vehemently anticlerical, so much so that in 1819, two years before his death at the age of 26, he objected to staying in Bishopsteignton, Devon.[1] His anticlericalism figures, in fact, as part of a much larger unconventionality. Keats was by no means a-theistical, or a-religious. He was, though, rabidly anti-Christian.

The warm and overwhelmingly gracious *Letters* offer a clear picture of the man and the believer, a picture confirmed here and there in the poems. Keats wrote near the end of his life: "I think a malignant being must have power over us—over whom the Almighty has little or no influence—yet you know [Joseph] Severn I cannot believe in your book—the Bible."[2] To his great love Fanny Brawne, Keats showed more restraint than at other times when he wrote dismissively of "the blood of that Christ you believe in," whom he also disparaged in the "Ode to Psyche" as "that pale-mouthed prophet dreaming."[3] Although he professed modesty and humility in the matter of religious opinion—for example, early in 1818, he wrote: "You know my ideas about Religion—I do not think myself more in the right than other people and that nothing in this world is proveable"—Keats lamented, in 1819, in a letter to his brother and sister-in-law: "The common cognomen of this world among the misguided and superstitious is 'a vale of tears' from which we are to be redeemed by a certain arbitrary interposition of God and taken to Heaven—What a little circumscribe[d] straightened notion."[4] The little-known sonnet "Written in Disgust of Vulgar Superstition" epitomizes Keats's abhorrence of conventional religious practice—with a hint of the alternative that he would develop in "The Eve of St. Agnes" especially:

> The church bells toll a melancholy round,
>   Calling the people to some other prayers,
>   Some other gloominess, more dreadful cares,
> More hearkening to the sermon's horrid sound.
> Surely the mind of man is closely bound
>   In some black spell; seeing that each one tears
>   Himself from fireside joys, and Lydian airs,
> And converse high of those with glory crown'd.
> Still, still they toll, and I should feel a damp,—
>   A chill as from a tomb, did I not know
> That they are dying like an outburnt lamp;
>   That 'tis their sighing, wailing ere they go
>   Into oblivion;—that fresh flowers will grow,
> And many glories of immortal stamp.

In the letter to George and Georgiana already cited, Keats also waxed positive, sketching an alternative to "the pious frauds of religion": "This point I sincerely wish to consider because I think it [the vale of soul-making] a grander scheme of salvation than the chryst<e>ain religion" (I remain faithful to the poet's inconsistent orthography and haphazard grammar).[5] He proposes instead that the world "schools" and makes the soul, acting as "a medium."

> —I will call the *world* a School instituted for the purpose of teaching little children to read—I will call the *human heart* the *horn Book* used in that School—and I will call *the Child able to read, the Soul* made from that *school* and its *hornbook*. Do you not see how necessary a World of Pains and troubles is to school an Intelligence and make it a soul? A Place where the heart must feel and suffer in a thousand diverse ways! Not

merely is the Heart a Hornbook, It is the Minds Bible, it is the Minds experience, it is the teat from which the Mind or intelligence sucks its identity—...[6]

Keats obviously recognizes the necessity of mediation, and he finds "the world" to be precisely such a medium; he also finds praiseworthy the idea of a "grander" scheme than Christianity that defines itself by means of being the opposite.[7] Keats tries again to make his central points clear, offering, I think, a better explanation of the "vale of soul-making":

> If what I have said should not be clear enough, as I fear it may not be, I will but you in the place where I began in this series of thoughts—I mean, I began by seeing how man was formed by circumstances—and what are circumstances?—but touchstones of his heart—? and what are touch stones?—but proovings of his heart?—and what are proovings of his heart but fortifiers or alterers of his nature? and what is his altered nature but his soul?—and what was his soul before it came into the world and had These provings and alterations and perfectionings?—An intelligence without Identity—and how is this Identity to be made? Through the medium of the Heart? And how is the heart to become this Medium but in a world of Circumstances?—[8]

As Keats consistently expressed disapproval of conventional religion, especially Christianity, its founder, its fundamental text, and its clergy, he tried on different replacements largely of his own making. The "vale of soul-making" is perhaps his most extended treatment, but it pales as instance in comparison to a recurring interest and desire. A letter in late 1817 represents his persistent desire as well as the general form of that desire: "O for a recourse somewhat independant of the great Consolations of Religion and undepraved Sensations, of the Beautiful, the poetical in all things."[9] The same answer appears, with elaboration and clarification, in the powerful opening of *Endymion*, published the same year:

> A thing of beauty is a joy forever;
> Its loveliness increases; it will never

Pass into nothingness; but will keep
A bower quiet for us, and a sleep
Full of sweet dreams, and health, and quiet breathing.
Therefore, on every morrow, are we wreathing
A flowery band to bind us to the earth,
Spite of despondence, of the inhuman dearth
Of noble natures, of the gloomy days,
Of all the unhealthy and o'er darkened ways
Made for our searching: yes, in spite of all,
Some shape of beauty moves away the pall
From our dark spirits.

The young poet does not flinch before "circumstances," which he can neither control nor rationalize. The passage juxtaposes little less than the horror of present-day existence, with such sufferings as the man Keats amply knew firsthand, and lasting, sustaining beauty experienced and then enshrined in memory. The same "faith" is at least implicit in "Sleep and Poetry" (245–47, 255–93, for example) and in the epistle "To J.H. Reynolds, Esq." (67–85). Keats was never one to de-complexify.

In 1819, Keats sounds a very similar note, advising the victim of "the melancholy fit" to "glut thy sorrow on a morning rose, / Or on the rainbow of the salt sand-wave, / Or on the wealth of peonies," or, finally, to "feed deep, deep upon [thy mistress's] peerless eyes" ("Ode on Melancholy," 15–17, 21). At the end of his life, Keats was advising the same, *The Fall of Hyperion* renaming the effort begun at the beginning of his career as poet: indeed, Keats, who was trained as a physician, recasts the "poet [as] a sage; / A humanist, physician to all men" (1.189-90). Moreover, Keats now identifies the disease badly in need of cure as dreaming:

> . . .Art thou not of the dreamer tribe?
> The poet and the dreamer are distinct,
> Diverse, sheer opposite, antipodes.
> The one pours out a balm upon the world,
> The other vexes it. (1.198–202)

The poet, in other words, may—and indeed, should—speak of beauty though never without due acknowledgment of the ugliness that so often surrounds it. There is, or should be, no lasting effect of "The pain alone; the joy alone, distinct" (1.174).

The justly revered "Ode to Psyche" deals in part, of course, with the collapse of old religion, the days of "happy pieties" (41) being past, the old myths no longer believable, and apparently a more effective replacement: "O latest born and loveliest vision far" (24). Keats focuses here, too, his belief in and commitment to what intensifies life and makes it livable, a belief in direct contrast with the asceticism of the Beadsman of "The Eve of St. Agnes" and the representation of Christ in the "Ode to Psyche" as the "pale-mouthed prophet *dreaming*" (35; italics added).

"The Eve of St. Agnes" plays a critical, possibly decisive, role in the clarification of Keats's religious thinking. The poem has not been well served by its commentators, however. In the Victorian period the poem was widely thought to be simply "a gorgeous gallery of poetic pictures" and (so) to "mean next to nothing."[10] In the mid-twentieth century Earl Wasserman invigorated Keatsian studies by giving the poetry intellectual content and substance while improbably representing "The Eve of St. Agnes" as a poetic demonstration of "the truth of Imagination."[11] Not long thereafter, Jack Stillinger offered a much-cited counterargument: from a validation of the visionary imagination, the poem suddenly became a repudiation of the visionary imagination, with the beautiful young maiden Madeline now seen as a hoodwinked dreamer and the protagonist Porphyro as a rapist![12] Subsequently, I weighed in on the critical controversy,[13] and indeed I base my essential arguments here regarding Keats and his great poem on arguments first presented there.

In simplest terms, "The Eve of St. Agnes" represents—and is—an intense, delightful experience: at once aesthetically pleasing and intellectually substantive. With no less care than he bestowed on individual verses, Keats defines and highlights the approach to experience that lies at the poem's center. Probably the most important means by which this particular response is spotlighted and defined is that of paralleling contrasts. Central to the poem stands an intensely realized way of experience that is very carefully, and favorably, juxtaposed with other approaches possible.

The most critical of these paralleling contrasts is that of the (Christian) Beadsman and his way of life, on the one hand, and on the other, that of Madeline and Porphyro, with their sensuous and sensual pleasures. The Beadsman bears obvious importance since the poem begins and ends with him. In this "delight of the senses," where plentiful and highly charged sensuous and sensual imagery co-exists with equally plentiful and prominent religious imagery, the Beadsman represents traditional religion, specifically ascetic Christianity. Keats thus contrasts the Beadsman's Christian worship, on St. Agnes's Eve (January 20), with both Madeline's superstitious ceremonies and Porphyro's "religious" adoration of his flesh-and-blood "saint." Asceticism meets happy physical pleasure.

Obviously, the Beadsman differs from the "barbarian hordes" (85). Keats appears little more sympathetic to the "argent revelry" (37) in "that mansion foul" (89) than he does to the Beadsman, who turns his back on their thoughtless merriments. Still, the poem's narrator shows no interest in the opposite way of this "patient, holy man" (10). What the old man projects is mortification of the flesh and rejection of earthly pleasures in favor of preparation for the eternal, and Keats clearly prefers the youth, warmth, vigor, and delight represented in the Romeo and Juliet figures. Thus the Beadsman is first seen in prayer, his "numb" fingers clutching the rosary, "while his frosted breath, / Like pious incense from a censer old, / Seem'd taking flight for heaven, without a death" (6–8). After praying, he moves, "meagre, barefoot, wan" (12) along the chapel aisle. What we see there in the chapel Keats offers as an emblem of the Beadsman's approach to experience:

> The sculptur'd dead, on each side, seem to freeze,
> Emprison'd in black, purgatorial rails:
> Knights, ladies, praying in dumb orat'ries,
> He passeth by; and his weak spirit fails
> To think how they may ache in icy hoods and mails. (14–18)

For the Beadsman, St. Agnes's Eve represents a time for such meditations as the picture illustrates: "His was harsh penance" (24) on this most promising night. His is, simply, "Another way" (25): the Beadsman chooses to sit "among / Rough ashes" (25–26) "for his soul's reprieve, / And all night [he] kept awake, for sinners' sake to grieve" (26–27). Yet Keats leaves no doubt about the Beadsman. The poem's last lines are these: "The Beadsman, after thousand aves told, / For aye unsought for slept among his ashes cold" (377–78). What "a little circumscribed straightened notion" it is, wrote Keats in a letter cited above, to suppose that we are going to be snatched from cold death and delivered to a place altogether different from the horror of this world, where "hyena foemen" frolic and storms continually rage.

In striking contrast to the Beadsman's worship is the happy fulfillment of Madeline and Porphyro, celebrated in the poem's thematic center. Like the Beadsman, Madeline is engaged in religious ceremony, hoping to catch a glimpse of her future husband by observing certain rituals on the special night; she appears, in fact, devout and steadfast in her belief, not so unlike the Beadsman, who resists the alluring call of "Music's golden tongue" (20): thus "she heeded not at all: in vain / Came many a tiptoe, amorous cavalier" (59–60). Simply put, "she saw not: her heart was otherwhere" (62).

Religious imagery abounds in the description of Madeline, her chambers, and her ritual observance. Young and beautiful, she is "like a mission'd spirit" "With silver taper's light" (193–94), and her bedchamber is said to be a "paradise" (244). As she begins the superstitious rite, Keats says, "down she knelt for heaven's grace and boon" (219). While she prays, there appears "on her hair a glory, like a saint: / She seem'd a splendid angel, newly drest / Save wings, for heaven" (222–24). Stolen to Madeline's chambers with the help of the old crone Angela, Porphyro is strongly impressed by what appears before him: he, in fact, "grew faint: / She knelt, so pure a thing, so free from mortal taint" (224–25). Later, her ceremony not yet complete, and in bed, Madeline appears "Clasp'd like a missal where swart Paynims pray" (241).

In the purposive movement of the poem,[14] Madeline has become the object of adoration and worship, no longer merely the faithful votary. She continues to observe the prescribed rites, but her function is now largely passive. Porphyro occupies the center of attention—as passionate as Madeline is spiritual. "Stol'n to this paradise, and so entranc'd" (244), writes Keats, Porphyro gazes for a time on the clothes out of which Madeline has just stepped, listens to her breathing, and waits for indication that she had awakened "into a slumberous tenderness; / Which when he heard, that minute did he bless" (247–48). Porphyro then creeps from the closet where he has been hiding and proceeds to heap up a food offering, which spotlights the sensuousness enveloping the scene (stanza 30 is beautifully expressive of the sensuous ritual).

Clearly, no textual warrant exists for viewing Porphyro as a villain, despite Jack Stillinger's claims in "The Hoodwinking of Madeline." Both Angela and Madeline are ultimately drawn to the young intruder, and from the beginning the narrator expresses sympathy: "let no buzz'd whisper tell: / All eyes be muffled, or a hundred swords / Will storm his heart" (82–84). Later on, at the moment at which Stillinger charges him with the intention to rape the young woman, Keats writes: "Now prepare, / Young Porphyro, for gazing on that bed" (196–97). Contrary to some (Beadsman-like) claims, sexual consummation lies at the heart of the narrated experience—and the narrator simply and clearly approves. As Keats's good friend Richard Woodhouse reported in September 1819,

[Keats] says…that he writes for men, & that if in the former poem ["The Eve of St. Agnes"] there was an opening for a doubt what took place, it was his fault for not writing clearly & comprehensibly—that he shd despise a man who would be such an eunuch in sentiment as to leave a maid, with that Character about her, in such a situation: & shod despise himself to write about it.[15]

Having performed his own small part in the ritual, Porphyro moves to awaken Madeline: "And now, my love, my seraph fair, awake! / Thou art my heaven, and I thine eremite" (276–77). She finally stirs, but then begins to weep upon realizing that her dream has passed. Meanwhile, Porphyro "knelt, with joined hands and piteous eye" (305). After comparing him with the spiritualization of her dream, she cries, "Oh leave me not in this eternal woe, / For if thou diest, my Love, I know not where to go" (314–15). At this point, "Beyond a mortal man impassion'd far" (316), Porphyro proceeds to an act of unmistakably physical love: "Into her dream he melted, as the rose / Blendeth its odour with the violet,— / Solution sweet" (320–22). When the lovemaking is over, Madeline worries that the merely mortal Porphyro has simply used her, but he calms and reassures her in words that identify the nature of their experience:

> My Madeline! sweet dreamer! lovely bride!
> Say, may I be for aye thy vassal *blest*?
> Thy beauty's shield, heart-shap'd and vermeil dyed?
> Ah, *silver shrine*, here will I take my rest
> After so many hours of *toil and quest*,
> *A famish'd pilgrim,—saved by miracle.*
> Though I have found, I will not rob thy nest
> Saving of thy sweet self; if thou think'st well
> To trust, fair Madeline, to no rude *infidel*. (334–42; italics added)

And indeed she shows how far she trusts him, fleeing with him "o'er the southern moors" (351).

Noting, unlike other commentators, the predominant religious language, James D. Boulger has suggested that "The Eve of St. Agnes" represents a parody of the Christian ritual of the Eucharist, with Love replacing the Body and Blood of Christ in the sacrament: "By borrowing and reworking for his own purpose the central mystery of the Christian ritual, clearly removed from its original sacred context, [Keats] was able to use the Beadsman as a foil to develop successfully, in his poem at least, the *mysterium fidei* of his own sacramental universe."[16] Apparently Boulger believes that in the religion of Love sanctified by the poem essentially the same *kind* of thing happens as in that that it replaces: that is, a(nother) mystery, a "miracle," occurs. But it seems more likely that Keats uses the religious parallels and language not to indicate the occurrence of a "miracle," which he most likely did not believe in, but rather to suggest that for Porphyro (at least) this intense physical experience has itself become marked with religious meaning and significance. This kind of experience may be the most satisfying, the most effective, now that the old pieties are no longer believable. It is the phenomenal level that matters, not the spiritual (or not the spiritual alone).

As elsewhere in Keats, so in "The Eve of St. Agnes" religious meaning lies in, not beyond, the physical. As (further) proof, consider the ways in which the poem defines and emphasizes its central experience. First of all, the sensuous and sensual imagery complements the romance itself, helping to make the poem a physico-sensuous and -sensual delight. Keats also describes Madeline's undressing with alluring richness: her vespers completed, Madeline "frees" her hair, "Unclasps her warmed jewels one by one; / Loosens her fragrant boddice," and then "by degrees / Her rich attire creeps rustling to her knees" so that she appears as "Half-hidden, like a mermaid in sea-weed" (227–31). The effect is clearly titillating, and the narrator joins Porphyro in enjoying the sexual prospect: "Now prepare, / Young Porphyro, for gazing on that bed" (196–97). And then there is the beautiful, and daring, description of the intercourse: Porphyro rises, "Ethereal, flush'd, and like a throbbing star / Seen mid the sapphire heaven's deep repose" (318–19), eventually, as we read above, to "melt" into her dream, "Solution sweet."

While thus insisting on the feast of the senses, Keats works hard to ensure that we view the physical union and its attendant delights as something other than and different from mindless indulgence or animality. The "bloated wassaillers" (346), those "barbarian hordes" menacing belowstairs, represent unrelieved bestiality. The narrator says, these "let us wish away" (41). In lines he ultimately deleted, Keats confirms his view of the "Hyena foemen, and hot-blooded lords": "Ah what are they? The idle pulse scarce stirs, / The Muse should never make the spirit gay; / Away, bright dullness, laughing fools away,— . . ." The revelers are not, then, simply sensual; they are, indeed, barbarous: their "very dogs would execrations howl / Against his [Porphyro's] lineage; not one breast affords / Him any mercy in that mansion foul" (87–89)—except for Angela, who proves to be of considerable assistance, protecting him and guiding him to Madeline's chambers. Whatever the reason or reasons for their unexplained animosity toward Porphyro, the "throng'd resort" (67) is composed of "whisperers in anger, or in sport" (68), and Madeline finds herself here " 'Mid looks of love, defiance, hate, and scorn" (69). The last we see of the "bloated wassaillers" simply completes the picture: "That night the Baron dreamt of many a woe, / And all his warrior-guests, with shade and form / Of witch, and demon, and large coffin-worm, / Were long be-nightmar'd" (372–75). In relation to them, Madeline and Porphyro appear in positive relief. By juxtaposing the central love affair and lovemaking with the barbarian revelry, as well as with the Beadsman's uncompromising asceticism, Keats signifies that not just any mode of fleshly engagement deserves sanction. The presence in the poem of the Baron and his warrior-guests establishes Keats's interest in *defining* a particular kind of experience, one that, while being opposed to spirituality (alone) and thus physical, avoids the merely animalistic.

In Madeline's bedchamber, we may conclude, finding her "so pure a thing, so free from mortal taint," Porphyro realizes that something extraordinary is available. Thus, and significantly, in the striking depiction of Madeline at prayer, the two prominent strands of imagery, the sensuous-sensual and the religious, come together:

> Full on this casement shone the wintry moon,
> And threw warm gules on Madeline's fair breast,
> As down she knelt for heaven's grace and boon;
> Rose-bloom fell on her hands, together prest,
> And on her silver cross soft amethyst,
> And on her hair a glory, like a saint.... (217–22)

The moment is one of impressive possibility, intensity, and beauty. Without in any way hinting at any spiritualization of Porphyro or of any miraculous transformation of the physical, Keats paints this experience as bearing significance tradition-ally understood as religious.

As it happens, the religious placement that Keats proffers in "The Eve of St. Agnes" bears striking similarity to that described in correspondence with his great love, Fanny Brawne. In late 1819, he wrote to her: "I could be martyr'd for my Religion—Love is my religion—I could die for that. I could die for you. My Creed is Love and you are its only tenet. You have ravish'd me away by a Power I cannot resist...").[17] His and Fanny's situation appears to parallel and here match Madeline's and Porphyro's. Elsewhere, similar parallels pop up: for instance, the lines "To—" beginning "What can I do to drive away..." contain the notions of "heresy and schism" (25); in a sonnet written to Fanny beginning "The day is gone, and all its sweets are gone!" Keats concludes, "But, as I've read love's missal through to-day, / He'll let me sleep, seeing I fast and pray"; and in the "Ode to Fanny" appear such lines as these: "Let none profane my Holy See of love, / Or with a rude hand break / The sacramental cake" (51–53).

Another important paralleling contrast exists, although it has been little remarked, between Keats's great poem and *The Divine Comedy*. In Dante's understanding, love of Beatrice acts as mediation, or rather she becomes the medium through whom he ultimately finds his way to God. Porphyro's ascent from the Inferno of the "barbarian hordes" parallels, with obvious and large differences, Dante's rise to Paradise. Unlike

Porphyro, however, he must first undergo Purgatorio, a cleansing trip to the Kingdom of the Dead. Porphyro has no such intermediary "stop" and so experiences no *understanding*: no participation in the world that threatens and will pursue him—his heart neither healed nor heeled (which is what happens to Odysseus upon visiting the Kingdom of the Dead). As a result, perhaps, of this elision, this omission, this failure, Porphyro sees Madeline herself as God-like. In her, Divinity rests; she does not point to, or lead him, to God. What bears importance, in both the writing to and about Fanny Brawne and "The Eve of St. Agnes," is not, however, that a woman becomes a source of religious experience and the object of worship, but that the love situation appears as the supreme, or paradigm, of a spectrum of beautiful, intense experiences.

Furthermore, alongside this sustaining belief in intense experience that will make life bearable stands an equally prominent skepticism regarding the likelihood of any settled solution to life's quite often horrific problems (such as Keats himself knew firsthand). The insistence on cold and even death in the frame that surrounds the sparkling romance puts the story of Madeline and Porphyro squarely in a harsh, unfeeling, cruel world. The suggestion is unmistakable that beautiful, exalted moments are temporary and fleeting. In fact, as the two lovers are deep in enjoyment, a "storm" rages outside. Fleeing from the "mansion foul," they run directly into it. And as we have read, for all his piety and devotion, his abstinence and his faith, the Beadsman receives no reward in life; nor does he enjoy an afterlife: "For aye [that is, 'ever'] unsought-for, he slept among his ashes cold." Keats never lets his readers forget the real while, briefly, enjoying the romance, whose limitations he never denies, forgets, or diminishes.

If Keats believed so deeply and strongly in the consolatory and restorative powers of certain kinds of experience, it is likely that he considered poetry as having a place of importance among these possibilities. After all, as noted earlier, Keats regarded the poet as "sage," "humanist," and "physician," pouring out a "balm" upon a needy world. The presence of the realistic frame surrounding the central romance indicates at once that, in such a brutish world as "The Eve of St. Agnes" is at pains to depict, some kind of momentary satisfaction is at least possible, and that the spotlighted experience is indeed ephemeral. The constant pressure of the mortal and the brutish prevents any tempting illusion that paradise is available here below for us ordinary mortals—at least not for long. (This, by the way, neither the Knight in "La Belle Dame sans Merci" nor the bewitched lover Lycius in "Lamia" understands.) By returning to and actually heightening the romance terminology at the end, *in* the frame, Keats calls attention to the romance as story: there rages an "elfin-storm from faery land" (343), and the narrator speaks of "dragons" (353), "phantoms" (361), and "witches" (374). We cannot, thus, fail to miss the fictionality of the events just witnessed and enjoyed.

The "most heart-easing things" ("Sleep and Poetry" 268) come from poets, not "dreamers"; the latter "vex" the world by creating illusions, deceiving, *hoodwinking*. Poets, on the other hand, take full account and make ample acknowledgment of life's brutishness *while* finding something in the midst of the horror to bind us to the earth. As early as "Sleep and Poetry" in 1818, Keats knew that he had to leave behind the realms of Pan and Flora and come to terms with the problems of the world—neither "Cold Pastorals" nor seductive nightingales would be finally effective. He must pass up such joys, he wrote, "for a nobler life, / Where I may find the agonies, the strife / Of human hearts" ... (123–25).

In more than one sense, it is now clear, "The Eve of St. Agnes" performs the Keatsian function of poetry, pouring a "balm" out upon the world rather than vexing it. The poem graphically illustrates that some human satisfaction is possible, and in showing this possibility it acts as balm. As art, the poem is itself one of the "binding" experiences of beauty capable of filling the vacancies left by no longer effectual consolations; it *is* "a thing of beauty and a joy forever." Keats leaves no hint, however, that art is thereby superior to life, a claim that the "Ode to a Grecian Urn" carefully deconstructs. Art is consolatory and restorative, as well as limited: a conscious, fictional creation. Experience is all. "Nothing ever becomes real till it is experienced," Keats wrote in a letter, "—Even a proverb is no proverb till your Life has illustrated it."[18] For Madeline, real experience trumps her *dream*, for in reality she has Porphyro in the flesh.

Madeline does not lead the "famish'd pilgrim" beyond herself—*he* is more "hoodwinked," then, than she. Meaning, such as it is, briefly glimpsed, is, for Keats, completely immanent. The ultimate hoodwinking in "The Eve of St. Agnes" is of the layman-poet.

3

George Eliot's "Layman's Faith":
The Lyrical Essay-Novel
Adam Bede

Many if not most readers of George Eliot's *Adam Bede* find distracting and annoying not only the West Midlands dialect of the late eighteenth century but also the massively slow pace of the story, partly the result of obtrusive and irritating narrative commentary. Eliot, born Mary Ann Evans Cross, leaves little to the reader's interpreting, for her relentless and loquacious narrator constantly intervenes, filling in details, explaining, and reassuring.[1] Like other great novels of the eighteenth and nineteenth centuries, particularly in England, *Adam Bede* is a rather unholy mix of narrative and essay, the narrator the embodiment of the author's values, its "massive" slowness both reflective of the era in which it takes place and indicative of a way of life—in harmony with nature—that George Eliot prizes and sets against more modern times. The narrator's running commentary, epitomized in the seventeenth chapter unabashedly titled "In Which the Story Pauses a Little," becomes so important a part of the total narrative that we (may) finally recognize that the work before us, in fact, is both novel and essay. In its thematic focus, if not also its artistic strategies, *Adam Bede* offers an important slant on the layman's faith and so the relation of religion and literature.

The *genius loci* of this challenging and precarious effort—this essay-novel—is William Wordsworth, from whom the author draws for her epigraph and whose revolutionary *Lyrical Ballads* is cited early on (73).[2] The bulk of the story is set in 1799, a year after the publication of that collection of poems that ushered in the Romantic period. Eliot makes a strong point of juxtaposing Romantic values with those more hardened Victorian ones of the time at which she is writing, the late-1850s. The difference that makes forms much of the drama here, and Eliot's narrator preaches about the newer viewpoint, the decline in human feeling, and the actual regress in sensibility (see, for example, 76). In the Preface to *Lyrical Ballads*, Wordsworth described his (and his friend Coleridge's) poems as "short essays";[3] *Adam Bede* is a far longer essay at once lyrical and critical in nature. The narrator may not exactly serve as hero here—there is, after all, the title character as "the new Adam"—as in Flaubert's *Madame Bovary*, whose opening word (*"Nous"*) points, brilliantly, to the narrator's physical and literal involvement in the story, an integument that but for a single later and minor reappearance efficiently poses the necessary questions; but Eliot's "voice" represents the essential values.

The story is a good, though simple, one. It resembles, in important ways, the more famous novel that came out the same year, Nathaniel Hawthorne's *The Scarlet Letter*, which has, in fact, a similar plot of Fall and its consequences, and has a couple of characters with startlingly similar names. Adam's story is, in any case, a kind of *Bildungsroman*. Other characters central to Adam's developing education include Hetty Sorrel (cf. Hester Pyrnne), the beautiful young girl whom he (thinks he) loves, but who gets herself pregnant by the Squire's son, Captain Arthur Donnithorne (cf. Arthur Dimmesdale); and the plain-spoken and earnest Methodist preacher, Dinah Morris, Hetty's sister (and opposite), whom Adam's sentimental and soft brother Seth loves but in the end loses to Adam (of course). Eliot enriches the texture of her novel with a set of supporting characters including the Poysers, aunt and uncle of Hetty and Dinah; the Bede mother, Lizbeth; the schoolteacher Bartle Massey and his symbolic dog Vixen; and the Rector of Broxton, the Rev. Mr. Irwine, "with whom," writes Eliot, "I desire you to be in perfect charity, far as he may be from satisfying your demands on the clerical character" (178).

Nowhere is the narrator's voice more important, or effective, than in Chapter 17, which is a brilliant set piece—essay, really—on Dutch genre painting, the ordinary life, and the meaning and significance of the commonplace. Following a chapter titled, simply, "Links," which itself follows "The Two Bed-Chambers," Eliot opens with the imagined response of one of her readers to an important moment in the narrative: "This Rector of Broxton," the Reverend Mr. Irwine, "is little better than a pagan!" The battle is thus joined. "How much more edifying it would have been if you had made him give Arthur some truly spiritual advice! You might have put into his mouth the most beautiful things—quite as good as reading a sermon" (174). Several points are raised here: questions of what is "edifying," the relation of fiction and sermon and so of literature and religion, the general, inclusive matter of truth and its conveyance—large issues, indeed, in a work in which the novelist tells the reader plainly: "We are children of a large family, and must learn, as such children do, not to expect that our hurts will be made too much of—to be content with little nurture and caressing, and help each other the more" (282).

The circumstances of the Rev. Mr. Adolphus Irwine, erstwhile Rector of Broxton, provides the opportunity for George Eliot to expatiate fully on complexity, fidelity to reality, and narrative art. Thus she writes, in the second paragraph of Chapter 17:

Certainly I could [accept her imagined reader's demand] if I held it the highest vocation of the novelist to represent things as they never have been and never will be. Then, of course, I might re-fashion life and character entirely after my own liking; I might select the most unexceptionable type of clergyman and put my own admirable opinions into his mouth on all occasions. But it happens, on the contrary, that my strongest effort is to avoid any such arbitrary picture, and to give a faithful account of men and things as they have mirrored themselves in my mind. The mirror is doubtless defective; the outlines will sometimes be disturbed, the reflection faint or confused; but I feel as much bound to tell you as precisely as I can what that reflection is, as if I were in the witness-box, narrating my experience on oath. (174)

The passage no doubt recalls Wordsworth, defending his manner and subject matter in *Lyrical Ballads*. It also allows Eliot to contrast the more "feeling" past of 1799 with the more "sensible" present of 60 years later. Whereas her imagined reader wishes to have expressed "those correct views which it is our privilege to possess," she refuses to "touch [the picture] up with a tasteful pencil" (175), writing, instead, and confirming the importance of Rev. Mr. Irwine and of clerical issues to the novel-essay:

> Sixty years ago—it is a long time, so no wonder things have changed—all clergymen were not zealous; indeed, there is reason to believe that the number of zealous clergymen were small, and it is probable that if one among the small minority had owned the livings of Broxton and Hayslope in the year 1799, you would have liked him no better than you like Mr. Irwine. Ten to one, you would have thought him a tasteless, indiscreet, methodistical man. It is so very rarely that facts hit that nice medium required by our own enlightened opinions and refined taste! (174–75)

Sympathy does not overshadow, or prevent, judgment.

Early in the novel, Eliot carefully introduces us to Mr. Irwine, representing him first, at home, in the rectory, with his mother and his sisters, for whom he exercises estimable responsibility. Although a minor character, Mr. Irwine bears a heavy thematic burden, representing a clergyman's faith. Eliot herself cares deeply for him, presenting him in a fair and balanced manner. "See," she writes, "the difference between the impression a man makes on you when you walk by his side in familiar talk, or look at him in his home, and the figure he makes when seen from a lofty historical level, or even in the eyes of a critical neighbour who thinks of him as an embodied system of opinion rather than as a man" (75)—it is as a man that George Eliot thinks of him. Mr. Irwine is neither earnest nor moralistic or thoroughgoing, and Eliot strips him of his vestments to present him as a man, fallible, with warts and all. Setting him up thematically, Eliot says, in "The Rector," she virtually identifies herself with him in spite of his ecclesiastical position, with which she had little in common:

> If I were seriously questioned, I should be obliged to confess that he felt no serious alarms about the souls of his parishioners, and would have thought it a mere loss of time to talk in a doctrinal and awakening manner to old "Feyther Taft," or even to Chad Cranage the blacksmith. If he had been in the habit of speaking theoretically, he would perhaps have said that the only healthy form religion could take in such minds was that of certain dim but strong emotions, suffusing themselves as a hallowing influence over the family affections and neighbourly duties. He thought the custom of baptism more important than its doctrine, and that the religious benefits the peasant drew from the church where his fathers worshipped and the sacred piece of turf where they lay buried were but slightly dependent on a clear understanding of the Liturgy or the sermon. (76)

I am reminded of what the Anglican convert, poet, and critic Donald Davie says in *These the Companions*: "what matters is the physical act of worship, not the mental act of belief or assent" (170).[4] Eliot proceeds with her initial portrait of Mr. Irwine, distinguishing pointedly between the Victorian period in which she writes and the Romantic period in which her story is set:

> Clearly the rector was not what is called in these days an "earnest" man: he was fonder of church history than of divinity, and had much more insight into men's characters than interest in their opinions; he was neither laborious, nor obviously self-denying, nor very copious in alms-giving, and his theology, you perceive, was lax. His mental palate, indeed, was rather pagan, and found a savouriness in a quotation from Sophocles or Theocritus that was quite absent from any text in Isaiah or Amos. But if you feed your young setter on raw flesh, how can you wonder at its retaining a relish for uncooked partridge in after-life? And Mr. Irwine's recollections of young enthusiasm and ambition were all associated with poetry and ethics that lay aloof from the Bible. (76)

Admitting "an affectionate partiality towards the rector's memory" (76), Eliot proceeds to this praise that may appear stinting only if we ignore the novelist's interests in the difference that time makes: "he was not vindictive—and some philanthropists have been so;…he was not intolerant—and there is a rumour that some zealous theologians have not been altogether free from that blemish" (76–77); he had, moreover, what the novel educates Adam Bede into, and perhaps the reader too, "that charity which has sometimes been lacking to very illustrious virtue—he was *tender to other men's failings, and unwilling to impute evil*" (77; italics added), ample evidence of which the novel eventually provides. In any case, concludes Eliot, "it is better sometimes *not* to follow great reformers of abuses beyond the threshold of their homes," and in the case of the Rev. Mr. Adolphus Irwine, Rector of Broxton, "however ill he harmonized with sound theories of the clerical office, he somehow harmonized extremely well with that peaceful landscape" (77). Constantly drawing her metaphors and images from that landscape and natural life (see, for instance, 154), Eliot could hardly offer greater praise. The Rev. Mr. Irwine matters more than as clergyman—a layman in disguise, perhaps.

Eliot's demonstrative response to the Rector includes, as I have said, her pointing out the difference between the time of her story—1799—and that of her commentary: 60 years (see, for instance, 106, 164), during which so much has changed, and not necessarily for the better. *Then* the clergy were often not at all zealous. "Ten to one, now that we are supposedly more advanced, you would have thought [a minister like the Rev. Mr. Irwine] a tasteless, indiscreet, methodistical man." Continues the narrator, embodying the common sense *cum* sympathy so important to the story:

> …Perhaps you will say, "Do improve the facts a little, then; make them more accordant with those correct views which it is our privilege to possess. The world is not just what we like; do touch it up with a tasteful pencil, and make believe it is not quite such a mixed entangled affair. Let all people who hold unexceptionable opinions act unexceptionably. Let your most

faulty characters always be on the wrong side, and your virtu-
ous ones on the right. Then we shall see at a glance whom we
are to condemn and whom we are to approve. Then we shall
be able to admire, without the slightest disturbance of our
prepossessions: we shall hate and despise with that true rumi-
nant relish which belongs to undoubting confidence. (175)

Precisely such confidence constitutes the problem, not least
for the title character, who will soon undergo a "journey
toward understanding" that involves considerable suffering.
An almost impossibly upright man, Adam must be purged of
a certain pur-ism, must come to understand that life really is
"a mixed entangled affair," must learn through participation
in suffering, the point that George Eliot works hard to show.

Then, Eliot immediately proceeds to the question how to
deal with persons who disappoint, who differ, and who oppose
you. Her response is both telling and central to the thematic
and structural whole—hers is the voice not quite of a sermon
nor that of a novel but, rather, of some mixed entangled union
with the emphasis squarely on ethical conduct in the here-
and-now: the sermon secularized, the novel patently didactic,
literature perhaps both offering and doing more than formal
or traditional religion.

These fellow-mortals, every one, must be accepted as they are:
you can neither straighten their noses, nor brighten their wit,
nor rectify their dispositions; and it is these people—amongst
whom your life is passed—that it is needful you should toler-
ate, pity, and love: it is these more or less ugly, stupid, inconsistent people whose movements of goodness you should be
able to admire—for whom you should cherish all possible
hopes, all possible patience. (175)

Eliot is thus reflecting upon, essayistically, what Homer *shows*
in *The Odyssey*. She also insists on truth-telling, refusing to
prettify her representations. She then continues from the passage just quoted:

And I would not, even if I had the choice, be the clever novelist who could create a world so much better than this, in which

we get up in the morning to do our daily work, that you would
be likely to turn a harder, colder eye on the dusty streets and
the common green fields—on the real breathing men and
women, who can be chilled by your indifference or injured by
your prejudice; who can be cheered and helped onward by
your fellow-feeling, your forbearance, your outspoken, brave
justice. (175–76)

Eliot is also, of course, laying the groundwork for her lead
character, who begins "hard" and must learn to have "fellow-
feeling": in fact, at first, "he had too little fellow-feeling with
the weakness that errs in spite of foreseen consequences"
(206). As a truth-teller, Eliot nevertheless differs from Homer,
as well as the Modernists, in the way that she understands
truth: for her, it is a matter of fidelity, for instance, to time and
place, whereas for T.S. Eliot, say, it is a matter of accurate
observation. George Eliot is not concerned so much with
observation as with presentation; whereas the Modernist insists
that literature will now have to be difficult, the Victorian
novelist insists with equal strength that she must treat the
simple—as a way to deal with the incapaciousness she finds in
the "advanced" and supposedly enlightened world of 1859.
She continues:

So I am content to tell my simple story, without trying to make
things seem better than they were; dreading nothing, indeed,
but falsity, which, in spite of one's best efforts, there is reason to
dread. Falsehood is so easy, truth so difficult. The pencil is conscious of a delightful facility in drawing a griffin—the longer
the claws, and the larger the wings, the better; but that marvel-
lous facility which we mistook for genius is apt to forsake us
when we want to draw a real unexaggerated lion. Examine your
words well, and you will find that you have no motive to be
false, it is a very hard thing to say the exact truth, even about
your own immediate feelings—much harder than to say something fine about them which is *not* the exact truth. (176)

Seeing, then, in T.S. Eliot, is *stating* in George Eliot. For all
her proclamations on behalf of the commonplace, and for all

his apparent impersonalism, the Modernist poet is really more concerned with the "average" or "common" person than the Victorian novelist, whose agonies *as a writer* occupy center stage.

George Eliot it is who endorses Dutch genre paintings for their representation of plain and simple folk and their lives; she invokes these ideas to describe and explain her manner in this book. She begins with the pointed criticism that "lofty-minded people despise" such art; in it, though, *she* finds that quality, that virtue, that she admires most:

> I find a source of delicious sympathy in these faithful pictures of a monotonous homely existence, which has been the fate of so many more among my fellow-mortals than a life of pomp or of absolute indigence, of tragic suffering or of world-stirring actions. I turn, without shrinking, from cloud-borne angels, prophets, sibyls, and heroic warriors, to an old woman bending over her flower-pot, or eating her solitary dinner, while the noonday light, softened perhaps by a screen of leaves, falls on her mob-cap, and just touches the rim of her spinning-wheel, and her stone jug, and all those cheap common things which are the precious necessaries of life to her.... (176)

Pastoralism—and idealism—worthy of Wordsworth. Eliot's emphasis, more than that poet's, lies squarely in delineating and exposing "the secret of deep human sympathy" (177), embodied in the narrator, learned by her central character through suffering, and to be embraced and taken to heart by the reader. Eliot eventually rises to this crescendo, having extolled the beauty of "human feeling" and insisted that we remember

> these coarse common people...else we may happen to leave them quite out of our religion and philosophy and frame lofty theories which only fit a world of extremes. Therefore, let Art always remind us of them; therefore let us always have men ready to give the loving pains of a life to the faithful representing of commonplace things—men who see beauty in these

commonplace things, and delight in showing how kindly the light of heaven falls on them. (177)

After this highpoint, Eliot returns, rather abruptly, to the Rev. Mr. Irwine, with whom, you recall, she began "In Which the Story Pauses a Little." With him, she now writes, "I desire you to be in perfect charity, far as he may be from satisfying your demands on the clerical character" (178), about which she has long been concerned, her first book being *Scenes from Clerical Life*. Here, now, Eliot breaches the barrier, not just willfully but deliberately and strategically between life and art, narrative and commentary, by recounting a conversation she had with her character Adam. The topic is religion. "I've seen pretty clear, ever since I was a young un, as religion's something else besides notions. It isn't notions sets people doing the right things—it's feelings" (179). In the spirit of ecumenism, Adam had listened to "the Dissenting preachers," including the Wesleyans, who managed to gather to their fold his brother. From this experience came a new commitment, resonant with a "layman's faith":

> I began to see as all this weighing and sifting what this text means and that text means, and whether folks are saved all by God's grace, or whether there goes an ounce o' their own will to't, was no part o' real religion at all. You may talk o' these things for hours on end, and you'll only be all the more coxy and conceited for't. So I took to going nowhere but to church, and hearing nobody but Mr. Irwine, for he said nothing but what was good and what you'd be the wiser for remembering. And I found it better for my soul to be humble before the mysteries o' God's dealings, and not be making a clatter about what I could never understand. (181)

The narrator shortly concludes the chapter by averring that "human nature is lovable" and observing "this remarkable coincidence, that the select natures who pant after the ideal, and find nothing in pantaloons or petticoats great enough to command their reverence and love, are curiously in unison with the narrowest and pettiest" (182).

George Eliot's own position, exactly—as she works toward redefining, and deconfining, and in the process establishing literature as solid foundation for what has traditionally passed as religious instruction—her own layperson's faith. To illustrate his point, and George Eliot's, Adam instances the differences between Mr. Irwine and his predecessor, Mr. Ryde, who was "sourish-tempered," given to scolding, and spouting dogma: he used to call doctrines "the bulwarks of the Reformation; but I've always mistrusted that sort o' learning as leaves folks foolish and unreasonable about business" (179)—thus the deepest, most profound wisdom from a simple carpenter. Adam tells the narrator of the clergyman's doctrinal scrupulosity and failure of sympathetic engagement—indeed, the absence of embodiment.

In Adam's mouth Eliot now puts the values she wishes to inculcate in us, her readers: he has learned the value of sympathy and the primacy of feelings in general. Whereas Irwine's stalwart predecessor "preached a good deal about doctrines," he himself took an entirely different, perhaps opposite approach. The ensuing account shows the depth of Eliot's interest in delineating religious differences. The Rev. Mr. Irwine, current Rector of Broxton, turns out to be the opposite, a kind of essayist himself and an embodiment of his preaching. Again according to Adam, as the narrator reports from her conversations with him,

> ...there's deep speritial things in religion. You can't make much out wi' talking about it, but you feel it. Mr. Irwine didn't go into those things—he preached short moral sermons, and that was all. But then he acted pretty much up to what he said; he didn't set up for being so different from other folks one day, and then be as like 'em as two peas the next. And he made folks love and respect him, and that was better nor stirring up their gall wi' being overbusy. Mrs. Poyser used to say—you know she would have her word about everything—she said, Mr. Irwine was like a good meal o' victual, you were the better for him without thinking on it, and Mr. Ryde was like a dose o' physic, he gripped you and worreted you, and after all he left you much the same. (180)

A certain anti-intellectualism, evidently endemic to the "lay-man's faiths," can be seen here.

As Adam says, Mr. Irwine *incarnated* the truths he preached. Then follows a summary account, from Adam's mouth, per-haps the novel's single most important statement on sympathy and its superiority to doctrine, a virtual binary opposition (of several), in George Eliot's terms: whereas, says Adam, Mr. Ryde "preached a deal about doctrines," different from the Dissenters, among whom comes the Methodist Dinah Morris, the female lead, with whom Adam's brother Seth is smitten but who eventually marries Adam:

> ... I've seen pretty clear, ever since I was a young un, as reli-gion's something else besides doctrines and notions. I look at it as if the doctrines was like finding names for your feelings, so as you can talk of 'em when you've never known 'em, just as a man may talk o' tools when he knows their names, though he's never so much as seen 'em, still less handled 'em. I've heard a deal o' doctrine i' my time, for I used to go after the Dissenting preachers along wi' Seth when I was a lad o' seven-teen, and got puzzling myself a deal about th' Arminians and the Calvinists. The Wesleyans, you know, are strong Arminians; and Seth, who could never abide anything harsh and was always hoping the best, held fast by the Wesleyans from the very first; but I thought I could pick a hole or two in their notions, and I got disputing wi' one o' the class leaders down at Treddles'on, and harassed him so, first o' this side and then o' that, till at last he said, "Young man, it's the devil making use o' your pride and conceit as a weapon to war against the simplicity o' the truth." I couldn't help laughing then, but as I was going home, I thought this man wasn't far wrong. I began to see as all this weighing and sifting what this text means and that text means, and whether folks are saved by God's grace, or whether there goes an ounce o' their own will to't, was no part o' real religion at all. ... And I found it better for my soul to be humble before the mysteries o' God's deal-ings, and not be making a clatter about what I could never understand. And they're poor foolish questions after all; for what have we got either inside or outside of us but what comes from God? If we've got a resolution to do right, He gave it us,

I reckon, first or last; but I see plain enough we shall never do it without a resolution, and that's enough for me. (180–81)

Right-minded regarding so much, at least as the novelist understands it, Adam seems off-base in setting up the opposition between Grace and the individual will, closing it off at the end here with his entangled notion of "resolution."

The narrator then closes the chapter with a long paragraph directed against "that lofty order of minds who pant after the ideal" (181). Based on experience, she concludes that, for all its imperfections, "human nature is lovable," an important point learned, she says, "by living a great deal among people more or less commonplace and vulgar." Against "the select natures who pant after the ideal, and find nothing in pantaloons and petticoats great enough to command their reverence and love" and who "are curiously in unison with the narrowest and pettiest" (182), Eliot writes *Adam Bede*, constructing it in such a way as to bring out *our own* best capacities. Many of her points, certainly, seem attractive, worthy of the closest consideration.

"In Which the Story Pauses a Little" does not so much interrupt the narrative as deepen and extend it. The novel is, after all, also an essay, prone to detour, in no hurry, and virtually defined by its indirectness. Rev. Irwine plays a pivotal role in the chapter and in the novel—and not just because of his failure of mentorship with his charge, Arthur. As an Anglican, he contrasts with the Methodist Dinah; he (thus) stands for a certain sort of past. He also serves as a pole of both sympathy and judgment for the (all-important) narrator. Just as Dinah's evangelicalism wins out in the end, reading secular literature produces results "quite as good as reading a sermon" (174). And yet—this novel is steadfastly *not* a sermon, for all its apparent sermonizing. It is an essay, hardly a sacred work. Distinctions matter, truthfulness above all. The fact is, as Chapter 17 soon shows, the world is "a mixed entangled affair," and so it is extremely difficult to "see at a glance whom we are to condemn and whom we are to approve" (175).

Eliot's considerable rhetorical skills are massed toward showing these entanglements, and *Adam Bede* "entangles" us readers in its story so as to reveal just these complications.

In the chapters immediately following "In Which the Story
Pauses a Little," Eliot pursues differences, sometimes oppositions: first "Church" and then "Working on a Working Day."
These will eventually be followed by—most starkly—"The
Journey in Hope" and "The Journey in Despair." Some of
these differences Eliot wishes to complicate and interimpli-
cate, essentially deconstructing. These include, notably, the
harsh Adam and the never-harsh Seth, religion and work,
Dinah's religious calling and the domestic vocation, education
and religion, preaching and teaching—there are others, of
course, around which Eliot scrupulously works, including
contrasts between Dinah and Hetty, the Poysers and the
Bedes, Arthur and Adam, as well as Mr. Irwine and Mr. Ryde.
By novel's end, Dinah has chosen Adam, rather than Seth. She
has given up preaching, the Conference having forbad women
from doing so: "all but talking to the people a bit in their
houses"; thus, she is not being "held from other sorts o' teaching" (506). Adam's word choice here is telling: rather than
"preach," Dinah now *teaches*.

And, indeed, teaching plays a huge role in *Adam Bede*. As
the narrator avers near the end, thinking of Adam and "this
sense of enlarged being [that] was in [his] mind this Sunday
morning" (499): "The growth of higher feeling within us is
like the growth of faculty, bringing with it a sense of added
strength. We can no more wish to return to a narrower sympathy than a painter or a musician can wish to return to his
cruder manner, or a philosopher to his less complete formula"
(498–99). Adam's has indeed been a growth, a journey to
sympathy.

Adam's literal teacher is, of course, the inveterate Bartle
Massey, his bitch Vixen close at hand, the only female he can
abide. The narrator introduces him at work with these poi-
gnant and telling words: "It was almost as if three rough
animals were making humble efforts to learn how they might
become human" (229). He knows his former pupil well: "you're

overhasty and proud," he tells him, observing the mote or a bit more in Adam's eye while missing the beam in his own, "and apt to set your teeth against folks that don't square to your notions" (238). Of course, Adam has a bit more education to follow: the young coquette Hetty, whom he has asked to marry, gets entangled, outside her class, in an affair with the young squire, Arthur Donnithorne, the tragic results of which are, first, her pregnancy, and, then, her conviction for the murder of the unborn child.

On "the eve of the trial," the title of Chapter 41, Adam waits with—significantly—the schoolmaster. Mr. Irwine comes along and urges Adam to be patient with Arthur, his own favorite: he *will* suffer, the priest assures him, adding, wisely, "The evil consequences that may lie folded in a single act of selfish indulgence is a thought so awful that it ought surely to awaken some feeling less presumptuous than a rash desire to punish" (402). The message is pointed and clear, especially to us readers, that Adam's incapacity is just the issue. "Men's lives are as thoroughly blended with each other as the air they breathe: evil spreads as necessarily as disease," imparts Mr. Irwine, trying to teach the difference between justice and (mere) revenge (403).

The lesson of Mr. Irwine does not quite take. But on "The Morning of the Trial," alone with Bartle Massey, Adam has clearly passed through a "dark night of the soul." The narrator sets the scene thus; her point concerns Adam and Hetty, of course, she of the narrowest of hearts, now turned hard, evidently:

> Energetic natures, strong for all strenuous deeds, will often rush away from a hopeless sufferer, as if they were hard-hearted. It is the overmastering sense of pain that drives them. They shrink by an ungovernable instinct, as they would shrink from laceration. Adam had brought himself to think of seeing Hetty, if she would consent to see him, because he thought the meeting might possibly be a good to her—might help to melt away this terrible hardness they told him of. If she saw he bore her no ill will for what she had done to him, she might open her heart to him. But this *resolution* had been an immense

effort—he trembled at the thought of seeing her changed face, as a timid woman trembles at the thought of the surgeon's knife, and he chose now to bear the long hours of suspense rather than encounter what seemed to him the more intolerable agony of witnessing her trial. (404–5; italics added)

Eliot follows immediately with a sustained commentary that does more than put matters in perspective; she makes clear that Adam's has been a journey toward understanding—at least of "understanding" as "sympathizing." She necessarily speaks in directly religious terms of what is only now, with the schoolmaster present, taking shape and taking root.

Deep unspeakable suffering may well be called a baptism, a regeneration, the initiation into a new state. The yearning memories, the bitter regret, the agonized sympathy, the struggling appeals to the Invisible Right—all the intense emotions which had filled the days and nights of the past week, and were compressing themselves again like an eager crowd into the hours of this single morning, made Adam look back on all the previous years as if they had been a dim sleepy existence, and he had only now awaked to full consciousness. It seemed to him as if he had always before thought it a light thing that men should suffer, as if all that he had himself endured and called sorrow before was only a moment's stroke that had never left a bruise. Doubtless a great anguish may do the work of years, and we may come out from that baptism of fire with a soul full of new awe and new pity. (405)

Such describes Adam exactly, before and after. He then decides to return to court, along with Mr. Massey. "We hand folks over to God's mercy," he says, regretful that the Poysers have not seen fit to be sympathetic, "and show none ourselves. I used to be hard sometimes: I'll never be hard again" (408), thus joining his brother Seth in compassion and effectively deconstructing that opposition. The narrator reassures us, in fact: "Adam had been getting more and more indulgent to Seth. It was part of that growing tenderness which came from the sorrow at work within him" (460).

Eliot follows this remark with a long excursus on the power of sorrow and its indestructible life within us, chastening and deepening our capacity for sympathy, which she so pointedly honors. Work, for the new Adam, Eliot makes clear, is no longer his religion; it may as well no longer even be opposed to religion. "His work, as you know," writes Eliot, "had always been part of his religion, and from very early days he saw clearly that good carpentry was God's will—was that form of God's will that most immediately concerned him" (460–61). Adam has been reborn—or, rather, is in the process of being reborn, for Eliot insists, rightly, on the gradualness of that ongoing work. "He did not," says she, "know that the power of loving was all the while gaining new force within him" (461). Work now, in fact, becomes associated with just this power of sorrow and sympathy underway within, a new definition, therefore:

> For Adam, though you see him quite master of himself, working hard and delighting in his work after his inborn inalienable nature, had not outlived his sorrow—had not felt it slip from him as a temporary burden, and leave him the same man again. Do any of us? God forbid. It would be a poor result of all our anguish and our wrestling if we were nothing but our old selves at the end of it—if we could return to the same blind loves, the same self-confident blame, the same light thoughts of human suffering, the same frivolous gossip over blighted human lives, the same feeble sense of that Unknown towards which we have sent forth irrepressible cries in our loneliness. (460)

The truth that George Eliot embraces is putatively Christian but shorn of its Christian trappings, she makes clear, a kind of "natural supernaturalism," such as the one M.H. Abrams ascribed to the poet Wordsworth, who is always looking over Eliot's shoulder as she writes: "Let us rather be thankful that our sorrow lives in us as an indestructible force, only changing its form, as forces do, and passing from pain into sympathy—the one poor word which includes all our best insight and our best love" (ibid.). Then Eliot repeats that these forces are continuing to work within Adam—there is, and has been, no sudden, immediate, complete transformation:

> Not that this transformation of pain into sympathy had completely taken place in Adam yet. There was still a great remnant of pain, and this he felt would subsist as long as *her* pain was not a memory, but an existing thing, which he must think of as renewed with the light of every new morning. (ibid.)

For Adam, there soon comes "a resurrection of his dead joy" (472).

The problem on which the novel focuses—that insufficiency of fellow feeling such that we poor forked creatures do not sympathize enough with our fallible fellow human beings when they fall, as they inevitably do—is mirrored in Hetty Sorrel. She falls farthest and hardest, "in spite of foreseen consequences." Nowhere is George Eliot clearer than in the following editorial commentary about the failure of religion as traditionally defined to prevent such catastrophes and tragedies:

> Religious doctrines had taken no hold on Hetty's mind. She was one of those numerous people who have had godfathers and godmothers, learned their catechism, been confirmed, and gone to church every Sunday, and yet, for any *practical result of strength in life*, or trust in death, have never appropriated a single Christian idea or Christian feeling. You would misunderstand her thoughts during these wretched days, if you imagined that they were influenced either by religious fears or religious hopes. (366; italics added)

In such a situation (even) Mr. Irwine's pastoral care matters not as a reflection of religion but as simple, plain human fellow feeling, the only effective way, Eliot shows, of surviving and finding joy in this "mixed entangled affair" that is human existence. Thus it is that the novel closes with Dinah no longer preaching. Instead, she is married, is a mother, and continues to minister to people *outside* the confines of religion.

It is important to pinpoint what it is that George Eliot is advancing here. First, a necessary distinction: with close and scrupulous attention to Old Testament writings, particularly those detailing their enslavement, Cynthia Ozick has argued that the Jews "will not forget—not out of spite for the wrong-doers, but as a means to understand what it is to be an outcast, a foreigner, an alien of any kind." Moreover, she adds, "By turning the concrete memory of slavery into a universalizing metaphor of reciprocity, the ex-slaves discover a way to convert imagination into a serious moral instrument."[5] Leviticus 19:34 makes the point: "The stranger that sojourneth with you shall be unto you as the home-born among you, and you shall love him as yourself: *because* you were strangers in the land of Egypt" (italics added).[6] In Ozick's well-chosen words,

> There stands the parable; there stands the sacred metaphor of belonging, one heart to another. Without the metaphor of memory and history, we cannot imagine the life of the Other. We cannot imagine what it is to be someone else. Metaphor is the reciprocal agent, the universalizing force: it makes possible the power to envision the stranger's heart.[7]

Powerful, this comes from someone who describes herself in "The Riddle of the Ordinary" as "stiff-necked," rejecting as she does any notion of a saving mediator: "the Creator is incarnate in nothing."[8]

Comparison allows us better to understand Eliot's position. Her interests are quite specific: in that "charity" that produces "tenderness for other men's failings." Adam's dark night of the soul and the morning after (help to) turn his hard heart softer. There occurs no large-scale shift in *understanding* such as the one Homer suggests and that T.S. Eliot explores. Adam gradually learns to sympathize because he suffers. There is no indication that he comes, thereby, to "envision the stranger's heart." He may, and does, sympathize with Hetty, even Arthur, and certainly his own brother, but it is primarily because his own suffering, by itself, tenderizes him. We are told of a broad-ening vision, but if there is, it appears in confined spaces.

Adam Bede raises, insistently, I would argue, crucial questions regarding sympathy and understanding—and poses them to the reader. The terms are not synonyms, although they are closely related; the latter forms part of the former along with comprehension. In this novel, with its strong thematic and rhetorical focus on sympathy, the question arises, particularly in light of the critique I have just represented, of its exact relation to understanding, which George Eliot obviously downplays. Adam comes to increased, and apparently sufficient and effective, "fellow feeling," but how much does he comprehend, and so understand, including about those around him, such as his brother Seth? In larger terms, does sympathy require understanding, through which it must proceed, or does the obverse hold true, and does it make any difference whether sympathy proceeds from sympathy or from understanding?

An outline for an answer might proceed somewhat as follows: based on a reading of Hebraic texts, notably including Leviticus, Ozick argues that sympathy results from being and participating in the experience of the other, either directly through memory or vicariously, through metaphor; that sympathy, in turn, leads to the "capacity to envision the stranger's heart." Christianity differs, of course. Understanding allows for Love, the latter proceeding from Being through the former.

In truth, sympathy, understanding, and judgment are three parts or aspects of one whole, although we may comprehend them as proceeding in the fashion I have just listed. To treat, represent, or embody them separately risks, at the very least, major problems—misunderstanding, in other words. Sympathy absent understanding risks indulgence; judgment absent understanding precludes sympathy and is almost certainly to be harsh, severe, and unfair. Comprehension and sympathy are part and parcel of understanding, which seems to denote at once and at the same time both what George Eliot calls fellow feeling *and* distance sufficient to realize faults.

4

Priests of Eternal Imagination: Literature and Religion—The Instance of James Joyce and *A Portrait of the Artist as a Young Man*

Stephen Dedalus is self-centered, self-absorbed, and egotistical; he is not even sure how many siblings he has; he does not listen, but instead lectures; he prefers literally loving himself to taking risks with a young woman, time and again—no participant he, in the world or the lives of others. Alongside this inveterate and confining selfishness is a craving for the spiritual and the aesthetic, Gnostic in intensity; the physical world sickens him, sometimes literally, and he flees its contact. Many readers, maybe most, consider him a Romantic and true artist, at least in the making, heroic in his defiance of authority and adherence to his artistic ideals. For his creator, however, Stephen is no hero, nor is he a valid artist; *A Portrait of the Artist as a Young Man* shows Stephen capable of creating only a *forgery*.

Strong words, to be sure, but Stephen evokes strong emotions. I have said in classes that I may dislike him so much because he is so much like me. However that may be, there can be no doubt that Joyce distanced himself conclusively from his autobiographical protagonist. This differentiation appears variously: Joyce changed his original title *Stephen Hero*; he carefully establishes, from early on, a clear pattern in

Stephen's response to people and to the world; Stephen's pen-ultimate and confirming diary entry, at novel's end, itself another authorial distancing, acquires weight from the appearance twice before of the key verb "forge" alongside the massive pride, egotism, and presumption: "I go to encounter for the millionth time the reality of experience and to forge in the smithy of my soul the uncreated conscience of my race" (253); and there is Stephen's highly symbolic mistake—and forgery—in recalling Thomas Nashe's "Brightness falls from the air" as "Darkness falls from the air" (232, 234).[1] Less clear, I reckon, is the way in which Joyce represents Stephen's continuation of Wordsworthian Romanticism—Stephen's own hero is Byron; that is, the young rebel rejects Mother Church, his Mother Country, and his biological mother (Mary), but his mind remains saturated with the imagery and language of religion and especially Catholicism. In short, Stephen empties religion of its content, retaining the vestments and creating a new priesthood ("of eternal imagination" [221]), thus reinventing the relationship of art and religion intertwined since his beloved Greeks. Romantic art and aesthetic replaces the Church, that "dying nurse" that Eliot describes in *Four Quartets*. Even I, with my intense dislike of Stephen verging on hatred, side with Stephen when he declines to join that priesthood represented in *A Portrait of the Artist as a Young Man* as saddled with only "the discharging of a formal rite" (221) and now separated by the lure of political involvement. Surely Joyce applauds Stephen's decision, at least the negative side if not also the creative and positive side?

Stephen's "journey" here—the novel, inter alia, a *Bildungsroman*—is mental and spiritual rather than spatial and geographical. In Joyce's next novel, the even greater *Ulysses*, Stephen's story is directly mapped and patterned on *The Odyssey*, on the search for "the absent father." Stephen is closer to Gulliver, however, than to Odysseus. In *A Portrait* irony abounds, for Stephen experiences essentially no education; rather than learn and develop, he finds only confirmation of tendencies and prejudices. Rather than expand and become more capacious, Stephen's understanding shrinks and contracts; at the end, he shows perhaps even less capacity for sympathy than at the beginning, alone, sick in his heart, not unlike Swift's hack-writer in *A Tale of a Tub*—contriving another escape from the world that sickens him. Literally poor of sight, Stephen not only fails to see but misperceives and distorts what is available: rather than darkness falling from the sky, as he thinks, it is brightness that falls from the sky, according to his creator, behind him, critical yet sympathetic, keen-eyed in his own physically impaired vision.

We are justified in reading *A Portrait* in the context of the "journey toward understanding"—and not just *Ulysses*, with its famous early twentieth-century progress through Dublin, Odysseus's great, constricted modern world—because Stephen's is the story of understanding. Understanding is Joyce's great theme, in both novels, as a matter of fact. It is readily apparent in Stephen's penultimate diary entry, along with his echo of the Satanic *non serviam* (already pronounced, incidentally, in the great "fire sermon" that makes up the bulk of the third, and geographically central, chapter). The novel works—at least its "rhetoric" does, to recall Wayne Booth's well-known notion[2]—often by allusion, Joyce slyly and sometimes not so slyly providing a site of judgment that allows the reader to see his character *sub species aeternitas*, as it were, and to be confident in our sense of *his* position. In this novel, impressively, autobiographical to the core, closely paralleling events in the author's own life, Joyce not only puts himself in the position of his character, fully participating (until the end, when he pointedly steps away from Stephen, leaving him to speak directly, via his diary) but invites us—nay, requires us—to put ourselves in the position of both character and creator, and at the same time. In this way, sympathy and judgment are maintained—together.

What the finicky, isolated, lonely, and proud young Stephen wants—and needs—appears early in the second of the five chapters. We have already seen a literalizing of the dominant metaphor as Stephen became physically ill after being shouldered into the "square ditch" by his classmate Wells. And now we read:

> Aubrey and Stephen had a common milkman and often they drove out in the milkcar to Carrickmines where the cows were at grass. While the men were milking the boys would take turns in riding the tractable mare round the field. But when autumn came the cows were driven home from the grass: and the first sight of the filthy cowyard at Stradbrook with its foul green puddles and clots of liquid dung and steaming bran-troughs sickened Stephen's heart. The cattle which had seemed so beautiful in the country on sunny days revolted him and he could not even look at the milk they yielded. (63–64)

Thus Stephen's revulsion at things physical and material. It affects, colors, and in fact determines his whole system of relations, not least those he would otherwise like with women. It is "only amid softworded phrases or within rosesoft stuffs that he [ever] dared to conceive of the soul or body of a woman moving with tender life" (155)—and so, on the beach at the end of Chapter 4, he transforms the girl standing before him, perhaps urinating, into "one whom magic had changed into the likeness of a strange and beautiful seabird," with "ivory" thighs and a bosom like "a bird's soft and slight, slight and soft as the breast of some darkplumaged dove" (171). Two pages beyond the passage I have just quoted regarding Stephen's revulsion at the sight of "real" cows comes this equally revealing narrative statement:

> ...he was different from others. He did not want to play. He wanted to meet in the real world the unsubstantial image which his soul so constantly beheld. He did not know where to seek it or how: but a premonition which led him on told him that this image would, without any overt act of his, encounter him. They would meet quietly as if they had known each other and had made their tryst, perhaps at one of the gates or in some more secret place. They would be alone, surrounded by darkness and silence: and in that moment of supreme tenderness he would be transfigured. He would

fade into something impalpable under her eyes and then in a moment, he would be transfigured. Weakness and timidity and inexperience would fall from him in that magic moment. (65)

When he, a few pages later, encounters the girl on the tram, he resists her move, flees in fact, eventually escaping into his mother's bedroom, staring at himself in the mirror, and then writing a poem—a pattern repeated in essence in the famous and climactic beach scene, that of Stephen's "ultimate" epiphany. Stephen wants to be transfigured, clearly, but it is just as evident that he seeks, although he is quite unaware of it, Incarnation: an "unsubstantial image" "in the real world."

Thus, Stephen remains, throughout the novel, unable to put himself—to participate—in the position of an-other. He famously rejects his mother's request, near the end, that he take the Easter Eucharist, admittedly a difficult issue. To Cranly's mention of this wish, Stephen utters a *non serviam*, followed by his declaration that he neither believes nor disbelieves in the Eucharist (239). Cranly then observes, correctly: "It is a curious thing, do you know,... how your mind is supersaturated with the religion in which you say you disbelieve" (240). Cranly directly asks him whether he loves his mother and follows up with questions whether his mother has "had a happy life" and how many children she has had. So uninvolved is Stephen—except with himself—that he responds, pathetically, "Nine or ten. Some died." Cranly is not to be outdone; he continues to press Stephen about his mother, and with every word Stephen utters, as with every evasion he makes, his situation is confirmed. "Your mother must have gone through a good deal of suffering," Cranly ultimately allows. "Would you not try to save her from suffering more even if... or would you?" Stephen replies, "If I could,... that would cost me very little." To this unfeeling but revealing comment, Cranly responds: "Then do so.... Do as she wishes you to do" (241). When Stephen says nothing in turn, Cranly at first remains silent: "Then, as if giving utterance to the process of his own thought, he said" (ibid.), distinguishing between the heart and the products of the disembodied mind:

> —Whatever else is unsure in this stinking dunghill of a world a mother's love is not. Your mother brings you into the world, carries you first in her body. *What do we know about what she feels?* But whatever she feels, it, at least, must be real. It must be. What are our ideas or ambitions? Play. Ideas!...Every jackass going the roads think he has ideas. (241–42; italics added)

Stephen has, of course, cared quite a lot about his mother, more than once, and at different ages, wishing to return to her (and the womb). But now, clearly, whereas his mother carried him in her body, he is quite unable, and unwilling to try, to put himself in her position, lacking the capacity to envision her heart or to imagine what she must be feeling—she who, in the April 26 diary entry, is said to pray that he "may learn in [his] own life and away from home and friends what *the heart is and what it feels*" (252–53; italics added). As to Cranly's questions, Stephen never really answers, although he makes clear his fear of religion, and Joyce leaves us with the sense of the matter's complexity. At the end of the conversation, at any rate, Stephen imagines—not *understands*—that his path is clear:

> Away then: it is time to go. A voice spoke softly to Stephen's lonely heart, bidding him go and telling him that his friendship was coming to an end. Yes; he would go. He could not strive against another. He knew his part.
> —Probably I shall go away, he said. (245)

Before doing so, Stephen goes on a while; indeed, his conversations with "friends" tend to be either fencing-matches, with him parrying their thrusts, or else lectures in which he spouts his various, usually aesthetic theories—he knows next to nothing of "*Gen'rous Converse*," nor of participation. Thus here, he says to Cranly, the novel's third instance of *non serviam* leaving little doubt about either Stephen's perverted, Satanic (lack of) understanding or his creator's clear-sightedness, Stephen no hero in his eyes:

> I will not serve that in which I no longer believe whether it call itself my home, my fatherland or my church: and I will try to express myself in some mode of life or art as freely as I can and as wholly as I can, using for my defence the only arms I allow myself to use—silence, exile, and cunning. (247)

Of course, Stephen is anything but free, a being made by his experience and enslaved to the "darkness" that he imagines as falling from the sky. Drawing to a conclusion, Stephen insists that Cranly has "made me....I have confessed to you so many other things, have I not?" to which Cranly responds, "gaily," "Yes, my child." Stephen then says, before parting company,

> —You made me confess the fears that I have. But I will tell you also what I do not fear. I do not fear to be alone or to be spurned for another or to leave whatever I have to leave. And I am not afraid to make a mistake, even a great mistake, a life-long mistake and perhaps as long as eternity too. (247)

By this point, I hope it is sufficiently clear that Stephen is on a mistaken, albeit complicated and complex, path. For many readers, including the majority of my students every semester, Stephen is a hero, rebellious, defiant, an emblem of integrity in (supposedly) following his own way. The hardest way, though, said Joyce's friend Eliot, is the middle way.

Stephen's various lectures make clear his limited, and mistaken, understanding. For our purposes, the most revealing—and confirming—begin with his lengthy excursus, delivered before the impatient, Horatio-like Lynch. These are heavily indebted to Aristotle and Aquinas and explain why Stephen espouses them; they fit his psychological and emotional needs exactly, precisely what he uses these theories to deny. He knows practically nothing, of course, of the suffering of which he proudly, piously, and pretentiously speaks:

> Stephen went on:
> —Pity is the feeling which arrests the mind in the presence of whatsoever is grave and constant in human sufferings and unites it with the human sufferer. Terror is the feeling which arrests the mind in the presence of whatsoever is grave and constant in human sufferings and unites it with the secret cause. (204)

In other words, Stephen goes on, pontificating and officious: "The esthetic emotion (I use the general term) is therefore static. The mind is arrested and raised above desire and loathing" (205). Such has long been his aim, his desire, in fact, for just as "The cattle which had seemed so beautiful in the country on sunny days revolted him and he could not look at the milk they yielded," his heart "sickened" (63), so Stephen, recognizing his difference from others, sought transfiguration and transcendence:

> He wanted to meet in the real world the *unsubstantial* image which his soul so constantly beheld. He did not know where to seek it or how: but a premonition which led him on told him that this image would, without any overt act of his, encounter him. They would meet quietly as if they had known each other and had made their tryst, perhaps at one of the gates or in some more secret place. They would be alone, surrounded by darkness and silence: and in moment of supreme tenderness he would be transfigured. He would fade into something *impalpable* under her eyes and then in a moment, he would be transfigured. Weakness and timidity and inexperience would fall from him in that magic moment. (65; italics added)

Of course, when he does encounter someone, the girl on the tram or the girl on the beach, he flees, in the former instance heading into his mother's bedroom to look at himself in the mirror, and in the latter setting off across the sands, crying of his "deliverance" and ultimately lying down to love himself.

Lecturing to Lynch, who grows increasingly impatient, Stephen continues in the same vein, aesthetic now playing the part previously assumed, first, by his mother and, then, by his Mother Church—later his own art will follow the same pattern. His tone is professorial, insufferable, and priggish:

> Beauty expressed by the artist cannot awaken in us an emotion which is kinetic or a sensation which is purely physical. It wakens, or ought to awaken, or induces, or ought to induce, an esthetic stasis, an ideal pity or an ideal terror, a stasis called forth, prolonged and at last dissolved by what I call the rhythm of beauty. (206)

His villanelle shows his art functioning as escape from the square-ditch of a world that he imagines he inhabits, one that then sickens his heart: *"Are you not weary of ardent ways, / Lure of the fallen seraphim? / Tell no more of enchanted days"* (223).

Stephen does not understand, ignores, and effectively dismisses Lynch's patent carnality: to Stephen's rhetorical direction "Let us take woman," Lynch replies "fervently": "Let us take her!" (208). About female beauty, with which his friend is smitten, Stephen can only conclude, and lament: "That seems a maze out of which we cannot escape." Still, with the cunning of his namesake, he adds, in tones clinical and ludicrous:

> I see however two ways out. One is this hypothesis: that every physical quality admired by men in women is in direct connection with the manifold functions of women for the propagation of the species. It may be so. The world, it seems, is drearier than even you, Lynch, imagined. For my part I dislike that way out. It leads to eugenics rather than to esthetic. (208)

Of the arts, according to Stephen, "the highest and most spiritual," the one therefore best serving his needs, is literature, to which he gives himself. He concludes with this stunning, and now famous, declaration, reflecting exactly his desires and needs:

> The personality of the artist, at first a cry or a cadence or a mood and then a fluid and lambent narrative, finally refines itself out of existence, impersonalises itself, so to speak. The esthetic image in the dramatic form is life purified in and reprojected from the human imagination. The mystery of esthetic like that of material creation is accomplished. The artist, like the God of the creation, remains within or behind or beyond or above his handiwork, invisible, refined out of existence, indifferent, paring his fingernails. (215)

With exacting mock-heroism, Lynch responds, plainly, flatly, and with considerable rhetorical force, deflating Stephen and his esthetic bubble, "Trying to refine them also out of existence" (215). No more than Stephen is either "the God of creation" or the artist sympathetically engaged.

For most readers, the pivotal moment in Stephen's journey is the beach scene at the end of the fourth chapter. His fate has long since been sealed, however; the scene merely repeats the now-familiar pattern. Joyce's dramatization is nevertheless little short of brilliant. It is a devastating confirmation of Stephen's perverted understanding. Joyce works to ensure that we be fully aware of his character's Gnosticism. As we have seen aplenty, Stephen would become disembodied, if he possibly could. Here, Joyce paints the scene with particular attention to Stephen's "discarnationism," recording his sense of his "friends" at play on the beach:

> How characterless they looked. . . . It was a pain to see them and a swordlike pain to see the signs of adolescence that made repellent their pitiable nakedness. Perhaps they had taken refuge in number and noise from the secret dread in their souls. But he, apart from them and in silence, remembered in what dread he stood of the mystery of his own body. (168)

Stephen has no clue about who these boys are, what they are interested in, what drives them, unable, as he is, to participate

d tremulous and wild and radiant his windswept
)

understands all this as his "deliverance": "This
of life to his soul not the dull gross voice of the
ies and despair, not the inhuman voice that had
the pale service of the altar" (ibid.). Irony falls
upon further irony. Rather than Incarnation,
ls—because that is what he seeks, as willful
half the truth: not life, but the world of spirit.
diately following sentence renders his judgment
en: "An instant of wild flight had delivered him
f triumph which his lips withheld *cleft his brain*"
added).

he final chapter of *A Portrait* opens with Stephen
n emptied and forged Mass, becoming a "priest
gination." He eventually kisses himself because,
, Anderson says, drawing out the implications,
e Jesus."[3]

his third cup of watery tea to the dregs and set to
crusts of fried bread that were scattered near him,
the dark pool of the jar. The yellow dripping had
d out like a boghole, and the pool under it brought
emory the dark turfcoloured water of the bath in
The box of pawntickets at his elbow had just been
took up idly one after another in his greasy fin-
e and white dockets, scrawled and sanded and
bearing the name of the pledger as Daly or
74)

. . . .

ning, everybody, said Stephen, smiling and kiss-
f his fingers in adieu.

ind the terrace was waterlogged and as he went
y, choosing his steps amid heaps of wet rubbish,
d nun screeching in the nun's madhouse beyond

sus! Jesus! (175)

in their quite ordinary lives. Apart, alone, deeply engaged with his own difference, Stephen is locked in his own mind. Joyce will have little of it, offering a passage that, mirroring Stephen's thinking, utterly and completely devastates, clipping his wings—he simply cannot sustain the grandeur with which his thoughts are clothed, the prose mocking him by simulating his passionate flight of fancy—it presages, of course, his own literal flight across the sands about to be punctuated:

> Now, at the name of the fabulous artificer, he seemed to hear the noise of dim waves and to see a winged form flying above the waves and slowly climbing the air. What did it mean? Was it a quaint device opening a page of some medieval book of prophecies and symbols, a hawklike man flying sunward above the sea, a prophecy of the end he had been born to serve and had been following through the mists of childhood and boyhood, a symbol of the artist forging anew in his workshop out of the sluggish matter of the earth a new soaring impalpable imperishable being? (168–69)

Still in his own imagination, heedless of those about him, unsympathetic, disengaged, tragically detached, Stephen finds his formerly sickened heart now trembling, and he is close to realizing his fondest dreams: "His soul was soaring in an air beyond the world and the body he knew was purified in a breath and delivered of incertitude and made radiant and commingled with the element of the spirit" (169). Joyce leaves no doubt where he stands vis-à-vis his character, who is perhaps (a part of) his former self: "An instant of wild flight had delivered him and the cry of triumph which his lips withheld *cleft his brain*" (ibid.; italics added).

Then, suddenly, before him he notices a girl. Joyce introduces this particular event—or nonevent—often said to lead to Stephen's climactic "epiphany," by emphasizing his character's isolation and difference, as well as both his joy and his delusion, striking a powerful symbolic note:

> He was alone. He was unheeded, happy and near to the wild heart of life. He was alone and young and wilful and

wildhearted, alone amid a waste of wild air and brackish waters and the seaharvest of shells and tangle and veiled grey sunlight and gayclad lightclad figures, of children and girls and voices childish and girlish in the air. (171)

Stephen *sees* nothing, alone in his will-fulness—until the girl disturbs, momentarily, his revelry. Actually, Stephen does not so much see her clearly as, in his will-fulness, he transforms her from woman into a kind of creature or figure with which he can cope, one that suits his imagination, much as happened, we were told, with the cattle at Stradbrook, whose carnality he simply could not abide. Rather than assume a position along-side her, or attempt to understand her, Stephen, in typically Icarian fashion, stands above her, recasting her—effecting a forgery—by sprinkling shards of his own created light and (dis)coloration upon her and making her delicate, no longer carnal, no longer human:

A girl stood before him in midstream, alone and still, gazing out to sea. She seemed like one whom magic had changed into the likeness of a strange and beautiful seabird. Her long slen-der bare legs were delicate as a crane's and pure save where an emerald trail of seaweed had fashioned itself as a sign upon the flesh. Her thighs, fuller and softhued as ivory, were bared almost to the hips where the white fringes of her drawers were like feathering of soft white down. Her slateblue skirts were kilted boldly about her waist and dovetailed behind her. Her bosom was as a bird's soft and slight, slight and soft as the breast of some darkplumaged dove. But her long fair hair was girlish: and girlish, and touched with the wonder of mortal beauty, her face. (ibid.)

Reality loses out to imagination, observation to psychological need. The girl Stephen thus makes "pure," free of the messy mix and inevitable tension that constitutes human being, although his eye cannot but take in those creatures that the ordinary male perforce responds to—Joyce's own mixed description is brilliantly rendered. The site of voyages, of jour-neys toward understanding, the sea serves as a mere backdrop

here for Stephen, who, inst mits himself to *flight* from h ity equally.

Stephen's direct respon "Heavenly God! cried Step fane joy" (171). He immedi body aglow, his limbs trem called him and his soul ha to fall, to triumph, to recr basis, Stephen could only nook and lies down. Now nized "world" of previous "He felt above him the processes of the heavenly the earth that had borne (ibid.). Soon he falls aslee max befitting his inabil another human being.

On the beach, Stephe merely confirmation of h Eliot ponders the "inter for him, however, the "always already" interse here, now, everywhere. J heroic, deflating Stephe taining this kind of prefiguring his later " replete with religious "enthusiastick fit" that condemned as madness

His heart trembled; passed over his limbs heart trembled in an His soul was soaring he knew was purified and made radiant an spirit. An ecstasy of

breath an limbs. (1

Stephen m was the cal world of du called him upon irony Stephen fin indeed—bu Joyce's imm as we have and the cry (ibid.; italics

No wonder performing of eternal im as Chester "he has *beco*

He drained chewing th staring into been scoop back to his Clongowes. rifled and h gers the bl creased and MacEvoy. (

—Good mo ing the tips The lane be down it slow he heard a m the wall.

—Jesus! O J

in their quite ordinary lives. Apart, alone, deeply engaged with his own difference, Stephen is locked in his own mind. Joyce will have little of it, offering a passage that, mirroring Stephen's thinking, utterly and completely devastates, clipping his wings—he simply cannot sustain the grandeur with which his thoughts are clothed, the prose mocking him by simulating his passionate flight of fancy—it presages, of course, his own literal flight across the sands about to be punctuated:

> Now, at the name of the fabulous artificer, he seemed to hear the noise of dim waves and to see a winged form flying above the waves and slowly climbing the air. What did it mean? Was it a quaint device opening a page of some medieval book of prophecies and symbols, a hawklike man flying sunward above the sea, a prophecy of the end he had been born to serve and had been following through the mists of childhood and boyhood, a symbol of the artist forging anew in his workshop out of the sluggish matter of the earth a new soaring impalpable imperishable being? (168–69)

Still in his own imagination, heedless of those about him, unsympathetic, disengaged, tragically detached, Stephen finds his formerly sickened heart now trembling, and he is close to realizing his fondest dreams: "His soul was soaring in an air beyond the world and the body he knew was purified in a breath and delivered of incertitude and made radiant and commingled with the element of the spirit" (169). Joyce leaves no doubt where he stands vis-à-vis his character, who is perhaps (a part of) his former self: "An instant of wild flight had delivered him and the cry of triumph which his lips withheld *cleft his brain*" (ibid.; italics added).

Then, suddenly, before him he notices a girl. Joyce introduces this particular event—or nonevent—often said to lead to Stephen's climactic "epiphany," by emphasizing his character's isolation and difference, as well as both his joy and his delusion, striking a powerful symbolic note:

> He was alone. He was unheeded, happy and near to the wild heart of life. He was alone and young and wilful and

> wildhearted, alone amid a waste of wild air and brackish waters
> and the seaharvest of shells and tangle and veiled grey sunlight
> and gayclad lightclad figures, of children and girls and voices
> childish and girlish in the air. (171)

Stephen *sees* nothing, alone in his will-fulness—until the girl
disturbs, momentarily, his revelry. Actually, Stephen does not
so much see her clearly as, in his will-fulness, he transforms
her from woman into a kind of creature or figure with which
he can cope, one that suits his imagination, much as happened,
we were told, with the cattle at Stradbrook, whose carnality he
simply could not abide. Rather than assume a position alongside her, or attempt to understand her, Stephen, in typically
Icarian fashion, stands above her, recasting her—effecting a
forgery—by sprinkling shards of his own created light and
(dis)coloration upon her and making her delicate, no longer
carnal, no longer human:

> A girl stood before him in midstream, alone and still, gazing
> out to sea. She seemed like one whom magic had changed into
> the likeness of a strange and beautiful seabird. Her long slen-
> der bare legs were delicate as a crane's and pure save where an
> emerald trail of seaweed had fashioned itself as a sign upon the
> flesh. Her thighs, fuller and softhued as ivory, were bared
> almost to the hips where the white fringes of her drawers were
> like feathering of soft white down. Her slateblue skirts were
> kilted boldly about her waist and dovetailed behind her. Her
> bosom was as a bird's soft and slight, slight and soft as the
> breast of some darkplumaged dove. But her long fair hair was
> girlish: and girlish, and touched with the wonder of mortal
> beauty, her face. (ibid.)

Reality loses out to imagination, observation to psychological
need. The girl Stephen thus makes "pure," free of the messy
mix and inevitable tension that constitutes human being,
although his eye cannot but take in those creatures that the
ordinary male perforce responds to—Joyce's own mixed
description is brilliantly rendered. The site of voyages, of jour-
neys toward understanding, the sea serves as a mere backdrop

here for Stephen, who, instead of *setting sail* for home, commits himself to *flight* from home, above land, sea, and humanity equally.

Stephen's direct response is profane, unholy, decisive: "Heavenly God! cried Stephen's soul, in an outburst of profane joy" (171). He immediately sets off, his cheeks aflame, his body aglow, his limbs trembling. He imagines, "Her eyes had called him and his soul had leaped at the call. To live, to err, to fall, to triumph, to recreate life out of life!" (172). On this basis, Stephen could only execute a forgery. He finds a shady nook and lies down. Now he imagines the mechanically organized "world" of previous dreams and rises above all that, too: "He felt above him the vast indifferent dome and the calm processes of the heavenly bodies; and the earth beneath him, the earth that had borne him, had taken him to her breast" (ibid.). Soon he falls asleep and into a swoon that ends in a climax befitting his inability to love the body and heart of another human being.

On the beach, Stephen reaches ultimate insight—or is it merely confirmation of his desire? In *Four Quartets*, of course, Eliot ponders the "intersection" of experience and meaning; for him, however, the mature artist, meaning is incarnate, "always already" intersecting experience, at every moment, here, now, everywhere. Joyce's language modulates into mock-heroic, deflating Stephen on the page, who is incapable of sustaining this kind of sweeping rhetoric. Anticipating and prefiguring his later "swooning" comes this wild passage replete with religious language, surely an instance of that "enthusiastick fit" that the English Augustans exposed and condemned as madness, the work of the "private spirit":

> His heart trembled; his breath came faster and a wild spirit passed over his limbs as though he were soaring sunward. His heart trembled in an ecstasy of fear and his soul was in flight. His soul was soaring in an air beyond the world and the body he knew was purified in a breath and delivered of incertitude and made radiant and commingled with the element of the spirit. An ecstasy of flight made radiant his eyes and wild his

breath and tremulous and wild and radiant his windswept limbs. (169)

Stephen misunderstands all this as his "deliverance": "This was the call of life to his soul not the dull gross voice of the world of duties and despair, not the inhuman voice that had called him to the pale service of the altar" (ibid.). Irony falls upon irony upon further irony. Rather than Incarnation, Stephen finds—because that is what he seeks, as willful indeed—but half the truth: not life, but the world of spirit. Joyce's immediately following sentence renders his judgment as we have seen: "An instant of wild flight had delivered him and the cry of triumph which his lips withheld *cleft his brain*" (ibid.; italics added).

No wonder the final chapter of *A Portrait* opens with Stephen performing an emptied and forged Mass, becoming a "priest of eternal imagination." He eventually kisses himself because, as Chester G. Anderson says, drawing out the implications, "he has *become* Jesus."[3]

> He drained his third cup of watery tea to the dregs and set to chewing the crusts of fried bread that were scattered near him, staring into the dark pool of the jar. The yellow dripping had been scooped out like a boghole, and the pool under it brought back to his memory the dark turfcoloured water of the bath in Clongowes. The box of pawntickets at his elbow had just been rifled and he took up idly one after another in his greasy fingers the blue and white dockets, scrawled and sanded and creased and bearing the name of the pledger as Daly or MacEvoy. (174)
>
> . . . .
>
> —Good morning, everybody, said Stephen, smiling and kissing the tips of his fingers in adieu.
>
> The lane behind the terrace was waterlogged and as he went down it slowly, choosing his steps amid heaps of wet rubbish, he heard a mad nun screeching in the nun's madhouse beyond the wall.
>
> —Jesus! O Jesus! Jesus! (175)

According to Anderson, "The nun's ejaculation suggests both a thanksgiving for the 'Mass' just ended and a naming of Stephen as Jesus."[4]

Stephen's attraction to the Church makes perfect sense, in spite of the anticlerical effects of the demythologizing Christmas dinner in the first chapter, when he is home from his first term at Clongowes. In fact, we learn from the narrator of Stephen's attraction to "the vague acts of the priesthood which pleased him by reason of their semblance of reality and of their distance from it" (158). If only he could have grasped what lay before him as understanding! But instead, he flees from that kind of tension, from the both/and that is Christianity.

Whether or not the Church, Stephen is certainly justified in rejecting the priesthood—precisely because it is no *vocation* for him. His pride and the prospect of power are the only bases for his even considering it. What attracts him in the powerful sermon that comprises most of the central chapter is what also repulses him: the priest, delivering a *retreat* sermon, appeals to the boys' fear. The sermon is beautifully organized but horrible in imagery and unforgiving in tenor. The impression of the Church emerging here and from the all-too-human priests at Clowgowes, to say nothing of the political interests then sweeping through the clergy, makes less for corruption—as in the materialism embodied in Fr. Bournisien in Flaubert's *Madame Bovary*—than for powerlessness, perversion, and perhaps irrelevance. I find little sympathy on Joyce's part for the Church as it then existed.

The "retreat" sermon is a "fire sermon" (to invoke, deliberately, the climactic third section of Eliot's *The Waste Land*), the priest engaged in a "fire and brimstone" effort at instilling fear and disgust and therefore leading to confession, repentance, and conversion. Stephen certainly comes away affected, and temporarily changed; in the event, he becomes, in fact, an ascetic, like the Samanas that Siddhartha first encounters on *his* journey toward understanding: "He had confessed and God had pardoned him. His soul was made fair and holy once more, holy and happy" (145). The sermon does not, however, take, or at least its effects do not last: soon, very soon, "It surprised him…to find that at the end of his course of intricate piety and selfrestraint he was so easily at the mercy of childish and unworthy imperfections" (151). It all directly comes to this, a couple of pages later:

> Perhaps that first hasty confession wrung from him by the fear of hell had not been good? Perhaps, concerned only for his imminent doom, he had not had sincere sorrow for his sin? But the surest sign that his confession had been good and that he had had sincere sorrow for his sin was, he knew, the amendment of his life.
> —I have amended my life, have I not? he asked himself. (153)

The point is, I think, Stephen has often *heard* about Hell; he has not been privileged to visit it as Odysseus did, nor even to go through a structurally parallel experience, like Adam Bede's "dark night of the soul." He cannot, as a result, put himself in the position of one who has seen and experienced Hell, participating in nothingness as well as realizing that he indeed participates in the plight of common humanity.

The strange, apparent stream-of-consciousness with which the novel begins concludes, with this rhyme delivered by the richly named aunt Dante:

> Pull out his eyes,
> Apologise,
> Apologise,
> Pull out his eyes.
>
> Apologise,
> Pull out his eyes,
> Pull out his eyes,
> Apologise. (8)

Hearing this, too, is effective, with lasting effects on Stephen. His hastily wrung confession is but one later and important instance of being *forced* to apologize or "Admit." Dante's words are especially significant because of the intricacy with which admission/confession/apology is woven together with a particular punishment. That punishment is itself revealing, since Stephen from the beginning is plagued with poor eyesight. Loss of eyes is, furthermore, linked in Freudian terms with castration (and Stephen does appear to show signs aplenty of the Oedipal complex). Less specifically, as well as less controversially perhaps, we may be justified in observing the figurative loss of seeing—that is, understanding—that failure to "apologise" portends. In any case, and ironically if we think of Dante's great poem *The Divine Comedy* with its message over the portal in the *Inferno*, Hell is represented in Stephen's mind as no gift. Nor is it in the priest's as he delivers his "fire sermon," which does not *purge*, but frightens.

In a rather startling passage, in the fifth chapter, Stephen's desire is represented as a turning inside-out of the idea of the priesthood, to which he was formerly attracted "by reason of [its] semblance of reality and of [its] distance from it" (158). Joyce here reveals, as well, Stephen's coarseness, his pettiness, and his meanness, as they consort, unproductively, with observation of and attraction to a girl as girl and human being, a step in the right direction, beyond, that is, that quick and immediate turn toward transformation and purification in the beach scene, at the end of the fourth chapter.

> . . .he felt that, however he might revile and mock her image, his anger was also a form of homage. He had left the classroom in disdain that was not wholly sincere, feeling that perhaps the secret of her race lay behind those dark eyes upon which her long lashes flung a quick shadow. He had told himself bitterly as he walked through the streets that she was a figure of the womanhood of her country, a batlike soul waking to the consciousness of itself in darkness and secrecy and loneliness, tarrying awhile, loveless and sinless, with her mild lover and leaving him to whisper of innocent transgressions in the latticed ear of a priest. His anger against her found vent in coarse railing at her paramour, whose name and voice and features offended his baffled pride: a priested peasant, with a brother a policeman in Dublin and a brother a potboy in Moycullen. To him she would unveil her soul's shy nakedness, to one who was but schooled in the discharging of a formal rite rather

than to him, a priest of eternal imagination, transmuting the daily bread of experience into the radiant body of everliving life. (220–21)

The irony keeps on accumulating and mounting in importance, for in placing all his faith in imagination—the religious terminology is apt, given that that Joyce himself has used—in imagination, Stephen reveals the incapacity that imagination, properly employed, might have healed: putting yourself in the position of another, participating. Further, Joyce hereby links to bitterness, anger, and failure of sympathy Stephen's substitute for religion, itself a substitute for escape back to the womb, and his new (but actually old) "vocation," necessary supplement, given the perfidy of the sacred (as opposed to secular) clergy.

Stephen thence makes up his mind to escape, now determined, ever more sure of himself, continuing the pattern established long before. In so doing, he reacts, and decides, on the basis of his own psychological needs and intellectual and spiritual incapacities. The life that he dreams of creating—"out of life," he says, by which we understand "outside" life—can only be a forgery because he knows nothing of life, which is "sluggish," always "grey," brutish and bestial, full of disappointment, overseen, merely, by powers "indifferent" at best, who, like him, do not participate in his situation or condition.

Rather than a representation of an epiphany glorious and fecund, the beach scene stands as a fateful, brilliant parody. Stephen certainly does not enter into life, despite his repeated claims. Following his act(s) of self-love, he only descends deeper into himself.

> Evening had fallen when he woke and the sand and arid grasses of his bed glowed no longer. He rose slowly and, recalling the rapture of his sleep, sighed at its joy. He climbed to the crest of the sandhill and gazed about him. . . . (173)

In other words, he does not, as Odysseus had done before him, "make haste back to the light": "Evening had fallen." Nor, of course, does he seek to get home, which he has hardly known; instead, Stephen commits himself, newly renewed, to flee from his literal home—Ireland "the old sow," he says, "that eats her farrow" (203)—and all that it stands for. He has thus learned nothing new; instead, he submits, and lies down, to his own will-fulness, his own imagination—and fancy-driven "enthusiasm," concocting a forged "project." Neither sympathy nor control is evident. Stephen drowns, not in the sea, but in his perverted (lack of) understanding. Little wonder that his creator parts company with him some pages before the end, refusing to participate in Stephen's perversions and leaving the work of narrating to Stephen himself, via his diary entries, which function in the event as a kind of dramatic monologue: the prose of *in*experience.

Are we left, then, with an either/or choice? Either we applaud and support Stephen's decision to reinvent the priest-hood, essentially emptying religion of its content, including its dogma, and remaking it in his own image, according to *his own will*, driven as he is to escape the real world and especially its tension? Or, do we embrace the traditional, perhaps ortho-dox, priesthood, accept such teachings as they are embodied in the retreat sermon, and condemn Stephen's desire to "fly by" the "nets" flung out to hold him back and to "go to encounter for the millionth time the reality of experience and to forge in the smithy of my soul the uncreated conscience of my race"? I think Joyce insists upon an answer, *A Portrait of the Artist as a Young Man* willing a response.

Joyce's notion, or at least Stephen's, of being a "priest of eternal imagination" should be considered in relation to the post-Reformation direction of literature and religion. Luther's winning declaration of "the priesthood of all believers" had far-reaching consequences, not only opening the Bible up to Everyman but also revolutionizing reading in general and essentially affecting everything we do as individuals. Dryden said in his *Religio Laici or A Laymans Faith* that "This good had full as bad a Consequence" (399),[5] meaning that while he accepted and celebrated the new freedom he also feared and fought against the license that this new situation wrought. An entirely new sense of the relation of religion and literature begins to be felt and to be exercised; Dryden may not be the first to recognize the deep and wide implications for both religion and literature of the Reformation, but he is certainly one of the most prescient and clearest.

I want to return to these developments, from Dryden roughly to the present moment, developments that both anticipate and reflect Stephen Dedalus's sense of vocation as a "priest of eternal imagination." Necessarily, I shall be repeating some of what has been treated in previous chapters, but I feel it important to remind the reader of the developments discussed there so that we will fully appreciate what Joyce makes of his central character. I include some writers, and understanding, additional to what I have adduced earlier. I did not include these for full consideration because they do not, with one exception (other than T.S. Eliot, I mean), like those studied at length here, offer directly religious poems or fiction. I must hit only high spots, and even then I cannot pause, for space limitations restrict my comparison and analysis.

Dryden walks a fine line—a tightrope dancer—in *Religio Laici*, as he accepts the "priesthood of all readers" while expressing willingness to consult the Church. His is the *via media* embodied between individualism and external authority, the future and the past, Ancients and Moderns, a tenuous, difficult position marked with such tension as he evidently could not long sustain. Within a matter of a few short years he converted to the Church of Rome, whose authority he thought necessary to stem the tide of already-rampant self-assertion and unrestricted willfulness then threatening God and King alike. The great danger, Dryden recognizes, is the unleashed "private spirit" already inherent in and fundamental to Reformation ideology, but he also recognizes, just as clearly, that there is no turning back: what to do, then, given that "good"? His solution is moral and ethical, at least in this

Anglican poem, which is at once a layman's faith, an amateur's declaration, a "common reader's" position, and, finally, an essay.

Dryden's is a defense of religion by a layman. Of course, laymen had written of religion for centuries; what makes Dryden's *essai* stand out is that he writes of religion *as a layman*, that fact emphasized and impressed upon readers by the three commendatory poems added to and introducing the poem in the second, 1683 edition. By the time we reach Pope, some 50 years later (I omit his friend, and Dryden's cousin, Jonathan Swift since he was a Churchman), the directions Dryden both recognized and took were moving apace. Pope was himself Roman Catholic, and a layman of course, whether or not a devout one; he was certainly no Deist, although reason plays a significant role in the very act of defaming unbridled reason—but that reason seems less supple and elastic than in Dryden. In any case, Pope was, I think, essentially un-Churched, although not exactly alone in a land with an Established religion, for his closest friends included prominent Anglican Churchmen such as Swift and Bishop Atterbury and the Deist Viscount Bolingbroke, so important to *An Essay on Man*. Pope offers that poem as a counterstatement to Milton's *Paradise Lost*, a theodicy, designed, he says, to "vindicate the ways of God to Man" (1.16).[6] The poem is more directly than *Religio Laici* a paean to the middle way, famously expressed in the magnificent opening verses of the second epistle; in fact, Pope everywhere urges embrace of the "mixed State," the tension that makes for political and social harmony rather than unity, and the pattern we call Incarnation: thus we proceed, he writes in *Dunciad* IV, "to Nature's Cause thro' Nature led" (468), for "human soul / Must rise from Individual to the Whole" (*An Essay on Man* 4.362). Yet Pope seems practically consumed by the notion that the "part" must submit to the "Whole," always insistent that he is "Slave to no Sect" (*An Essay on Man* 4.331). A universalism thus appears in Pope's writing, absent in Dryden, who recognized the centrality of the issue and who, as Poet Laureate (and an "insider"), was obligated to defend the Church of England (28). Dryden posits the *via media* as embodied in the Established Church, but Pope, far less ecclesiastical and more secular, evidently found the Established Church just another sect, and understood the "middle way" as a capacity of mind available to Everyman.

It is a step—a significant one, to be sure—from Pope to Wordsworth, much greater, of course than that from Dryden to Pope. In a comparison and contrast of Pope, Wordsworth, and Dryden, Maynard Mack has said:

> Classical poets do not wonder at man: they may admire him at his best. ... [T]hey do not make him a subject of reverential awe. There is no more revealing passage (revealing of significant shifts in point of view) in all of nineteenth-century poetry than the lines in the *Recluse* where Wordsworth applies to his theme—man's mind—the same panoply of venerative terms that Milton applies to God. For the romantic poet, divinity and mystery exist in man; for the classical poet, they exist in God. It is no accident that the passages in Pope's *Essay* [*on Man*] which have been credited with "sublimity" refer to God.[7]

That is clearly if somewhat simplistically and piously said—Mack one of those Popeans that Hugh Kenner chided for pontificating from their "Natchez-Augustan manor."[8] The world changed with the Reformation, beside which the change between Pope and Wordsworth pales considerably in comparison, despite Mack's rather tendentious either/or dramatization.

M.H. Abrams has written much more sympathetically of the Romantics' "natural supernaturalism."[9] For Wordsworth, however ambivalent in his pantheism (and, at the same time, opposition to Deism), the natural *is* the supernatural. He spends his poetic career trying to find and describe the exact relation of the mind (or imagination) and Nature. At the end of his great autobiographical poem *The Prelude*, he seems finally to have found it, deciding that the mind is "A thousand times more beautiful than the earth."[10] He thus extends, far beyond and indeed counter to Dryden's direction, the free expression of the *layman*'s religion. Priests now seem irrelevant; the poets may be the "legislators," as another Romantic, Percy Bysshe Shelley, averred, but religion has found its place in the mind of man, perhaps *as* that mind (see Keats's "Ode to Psyche"), and that mind has little interest in a *via media*. Instead, imagination, creativity, and enthusiasm now assume primacy—exactly as Dryden had feared and complained. Observation thus yields to reflection, personality replacing the contemplative soul.

Ezra Pound was no Romantic—no ordinary one, at least—but he too was an individualist. He was also an immanentist, a pagan—and a strongly and devoutly religious man. Like Pope, he thought the world revealed—embodied—a moral order, the world "cohering," he wrote, a unity apparent that Pope might have accepted. His thinking was epic, in a way Pope's never was, also more worldly and carnal, given to the occult as Pope never was. In many ways, Pound appears a thoroughgoing Modern despite his immersion in and adherence to the Greek gods. Asked once by his friend Eliot what he believed in, Pound eventually answered: "Having a strong disbelief in abstract and general statement as a means of conveying one's thought to others I have for a number of years answered such questions by telling the enquirer to read Confucius and Ovid"; he added, "Given the material means I would replace the statue of Venus on the cliffs of Terracina. I would erect a temple to Artemis in Park Lane. I believe that a light from Eleusis persisted throughout the middle ages and set beauty in the song of Provence and of Italy."[11] In "Axiomata," Pound reasoned in this way: "The intimate essence of the universe is *not* of the same nature as our own consciousness. Our own consciousness is incapable of having produced the universe. God, therefore, exists," though there is "no proof that this God, Theos, is one, or is many, or is divisible or indivisible, or is an ordered hierarchy culminating, or not culminating, in a unity." Revealing his opposition to conventional, modern religion, he wrote: "Dogma is bluff based upon ignorance."[12] In fact, in "*Deus et Amor*," in 1940, Pound, not for the first or only time, lashed out at Christianity: "The idea that the love of god for human beings is a Christian invention is sheer hokum, part and parcel of the vast impertinence of the Christers." He said, too, "Calvin's god and the god of all writers leading to and descending from Calvin is a maniac sadist, one would prefer other qualities in one's immediate parenthood."[13] The very idea of the priesthood was, thus, anathema to Pound, who insisted on the simple, the direct, the unmediated, and the literal: "The religious man communes every time his teeth sink into a bread crust."[14] Communion, then, but shorn of all ecclesiastical trappings; the idea of the laity, or the clergy, was rendered moot, for there are only laypersons. Like Wordsworth, in some ways in the same direction, and as an extension and development of Wordsworth's emphasis on mind, Pound, writing in 1918, in "*Religio* or, The Child's Guide to Knowledge," defined "a god" as "an eternal state of mind," and said that a god becomes "manifest" when "the states of mind take form," a man in fact becoming a god himself when "he enters one of these states of mind."[15]

The sadly neglected Northumbrian poet Basil Bunting, who enjoyed a brief renaissance of interest in the late 1960s and 1970s, was early influenced by Pound, as he was by his fellow Northerner, Wordsworth. An enigmatic figure and demanding poet, Bunting earned Pound's praise for his precision; he was also scrupulous and committed to his art, inveterate against filthy lucre like his friend Pound. Though he wrote next to nothing about religion directly, you can find certain positions indirectly in his great poem *Briggflatts*, the name of a Quaker meeting-house that Bunting attended in his youth, and a poem that he, like Wordsworth referring to *The Prelude*, called an "autobiography." For all his interest in the thing-itself, in seeing objectively, Bunting contributed to the movement of which Wordsworth stands as perhaps paradigmatic. As to his religious thinking, Peter Makin has written well in *Bunting: The Shaping of His Verse*, relying almost exclusively on interviews—Bunting's understanding is precisely part of what Dryden excoriated in his layman's faith:

> When Bunting tried to define the centre of his religion, he did so in various ways. He spoke of emptying the mind of its usual accumulations, so as to hear "what [the Quakers] would call the voice of God in your inside." He said that to study the universe, in the manner of an histologist studying a cell, was to study God. He called his belief "an extremely pantheistic one"; spoke of "a kind of reverence for the whole creation" that one ought to have, which was "a kind of pantheism"; called himself a Quaker, and called Quakerism "a form of mysticism" that was "comparable pretty easily with an [sic] pantheistic notion of the universe."[16]

There is evidence, I believe, that Bunting, more so than any of the poets here considered save Eliot, practiced a kind of "getting out of self" closely akin to contemplation, a poet almost Janus-like, in some ways Romantic, in others stridently Modernist. In silence, in any case, Bunting would listen for God speaking through his own spirit, whereas Dryden, fearful of just that, thinking it, as Swift did, a kind of madness born of self-induced enthusiasm, listened for the word of God *in the text.*

With the mention of contemplation, we come to Eliot, the most outwardly religious of all the poets named here, the only one, perhaps, strict in his observances and committed to dogma as such. Eliot was a Churchman, although a layperson, of course (he delivered a single sermon, unlike Samuel Johnson who wrote and gave many, at Cambridge in March 1948). In fact, Eliot wrote much directly about the Church of England, in which he was baptized in 1927, five years after the publication of *The Waste Land* and three before that of *Ash-Wednesday*: prose pieces, many of them notable, including essays on Lancelot Andrewes and John Bramhall and tracts like *Thoughts After Lambeth* in 1931 and later ones on the use of cathedrals in England and the possibility of doctrinal and ecclesiastical reconciliation in South Africa. He was certainly not so prolific, or direct, on Anglican matters as the later C.H. Sisson, who bears the older writer's influence. Still, in *East Coker*, the second of *Four Quartets*, first published in 1940, Eliot pulls no punches in referring to the Church as the "dying nurse"—dying perhaps precisely because of her true nature, her "constant care" being "not to please / But to remind of our, and Adam's curse, / And that, to be restored, our sickness must grow worse."[17] We of course, Moderns especially, do not like the straight and narrow path nor much of anything that is difficult and demanding of us. Already in *Religio Laici*, at the end of the seventeenth century, Dryden lambasted the *"easie God"* of the Deists and mocked and roundly criticized those "forward-looking" Anglican clergymen known as Latitudinarians. Sisson would later take the Church to task for moving in a direction opposite that that Eliot describes approvingly. I would not be surprised if Eliot grew less and less sanguine about the role and power of the Church—of whatever sort—in the modern world; after *Four Quartets* he gave up the writing of nondramatic poetry and focused on specifically social and ethical issues.

The final poet I take up here, Geoffrey Hill, is, though not so much as C.H. Sisson, influenced by and indebted to Eliot. He has long treated religious and ecclesiastical subjects, figures, and landscapes—in volumes like *Tenebrae, Mercian Hymns, The Mystery of the Charity of Charles Péguy*, and *Canaan*. His poetry, as well as his collections of essays, is difficult, concise, demanding, exacting. He quotes Sisson as epigraph for *Mercian Hymns*, and he embodies what the critic Vincent Sherry has called a "Tory radicalism"[18]—Sisson proudly called himself a Tory, Eliot himself a "royalist." Hill, I think, represents in some ways a continuation of Eliot's Anglican depth—although he has lately written warmly of Milton, in both prose and verse (see, for instance, *Scenes from Comus*). Lauded by critics like Harold Bloom, Hill is widely regarded as the finest poet writing today. I find him alluring, with that difficulty that keeps you returning, for you know— even though you do not yet understand it—that something essential is being offered. Committed to Christianity, perhaps to the Church as well, Hill accepts the responsibilities and opportunities that the decline and near-demise of traditional, institutional religion present.

Hill directly recalls Eliot when, as Vincent Sherry puts it, his "verse taps the resources of multiple meaning in a word's past, just as it disturbs the single, customary sense of the cliché."[19] According to Hill himself, "every fine and moving poem bears witness to this lost kingdom of innocence and original justice." That is, "the refinement of a poem may serve to perfect and redeem a fallen language; the disciplines of verse may atone for the ills of a corrupted tongue"[20] (recall, in *Little Gidding*, that the "compound ghost" avers that "speech impelled us / To purify the dialect of the tribe" and that the poet, later on, refers to "The common word exact without vulgarity, / The formal word precise but not pedantic, / The complete consort dancing together"). In an essay titled "Poetry as 'Menace' and 'Atonement,'" Hill writes: "the technical perfecting of a poem is an act of atonement, in the radical etymological sense—an act of atonement, a setting at one, a bringing into concord, a reconciling, a uniting in harmony." Hill also "likens the pains of the artist to the suffering of martyrdom," which he regards as a "'pedagogy,' a 'scholastic process of training' like the disciplines of verse."[21] In fact, in the sonnet sequence "Lachrimae," with its epigraph from the Jesuit martyr St. Robert Southwell, victim of the Reformation, Hill "links the figures of martyr and artist," the former the model of the poet: "an ascetic meting out speech, as though on a rack, to redress the wrongs of the human tongue."[22] The description of Hill as artist and believer offered by one commentator marks Hill's belonging in the group assembled here—one who, as Eliot wrote in an essay on Pascal, knows enough to accept the inseparability of faith and doubt, not unlike the great sceptic (and father of the essay) Michel de Montaigne, son of the Renaissance:

> A genuinely religious man, [Hill] is a true doubter, a believer who disbelieves, who doubts, if not the validity of religion, at

least his own worthiness. When asked to describe his religious experience in relation to his poetry, he refers to a modern Italian poet's: " 'A heretic's dream of salvation expressed in the images of the orthodoxy from which he is excommunicate.' "[23]

Or as Hill says in his prose appreciation appended to *The Mystery of the Charity of Charles Péguy*, after leaving the Church, Péguy "rediscovered the solitary ardours of faith but not the consolations of religious practice."[24] Hill's stance is indeed based in difficulty: subtle, complex, deeply nuanced.

The foregoing, and perhaps especially the all-too-brief commentary on Geoffrey Hill, leads us to believe that Joyce might well eschew a simple either/or in favor of a complicated response to Stephen Dedalus's bold declaration to serve as a "priest of eternal imagination." I rather suspect, in fact, that the novel itself marks a certain sympathy for Stephen's desire for something different from and more effective than the then-current priesthood of the Roman Catholic Church, itself the only mentionable one available; even so, the novel is highly critical, indeed satirical, of Stephen's motives and, I think, of the substitute he defines, itself a "supplement," really.

Having reconsidered the tradition of laymen's writing *as laymen*, we cannot but pause over Stephen's by-no-means-surprising retention of the idea of *priesthood*. He stands alone, and in vivid difference from the poets we have considered, in both the degree and the manner in which his mind is saturated—and textured—by religion, its imagery, its nomenclature. He is, in fact, less radical than the poets.

Joyce offers, in *A Portrait of the Artist as a Young Man*, if not in *Stephen Hero*, a Romantic understanding of religion and literature and then subjects it to unrelenting scrutiny and critique. The novel suggests what the direction of poets' take on religion since the Reformation affirms: Joyce most likely would not subscribe to a "thoroughgoing" embrace of the priesthood; he might well welcome Stephen's desire for a reinterpretation without accepting the resulting "forgery." Joyce believed in the power of art; he was neither so proud nor so arrogant to believe, though, that he could "create in the smithy of my soul the uncreated conscience of my race," and he surely knew that that conscience had been created long since. No one, in any case, can *create* it, not even the greatest artist. Nor, if creation were possible at human hands, would it emerge from "the smithy of [one's own, private] soul." Literature or art would not, in other words, substitute for religion, or take its place—a major nineteenth-century idea, and desire—although it might be able to complement it, in ways that Joyce, like Dryden, Pope, T.S. Eliot, Hill, and some others suggest and incarnate.

5

JOURNEY TOWARD UNDERSTANDING: T.S. ELIOT AND THE PROGRESS OF THE "INTELLIGENT BELIEVER"

In 1930, in the preface to his essay collection *For Lancelot Andrewes*, T.S. Eliot declared himself to be "classicist in literature, anglo-catholic in religion, royalist in politics."[1] The description ignited a firestorm, whose embers still spark paroxysms of dismay, disbelief, and dismissal—and an occasional nod of understanding and, less frequently, of approval. We do not know why, we can at best surmise, about the path, the progress, that brought Eliot from the apparent disillusion and doubt of *The Waste Land* and "The Hollow Men" to the capacity, assigned to Pascal and his *Pensées*, to "fac[e] unflinchingly the demon of doubt which is inseparable from the spirit of belief."[2]

We have a record of Eliot's baptism in the Church of England, we know who his spiritual advisor was, we know who officiated at the sacrament of baptism.[3] We also know that his friend and employer Geoffrey Faber had published an important book on *The Oxford Movement* and was himself linked with Anglo-Catholicism, as had been John Henry Newman, of course. We know that Eliot studied Eastern religions at Harvard, along with philosophy, that he had a Unitarian background, and that he was both conversant with and drawn, willy-nilly, toward both Hinduism and Buddhism. We have a "sermon" that he "preached" in 1948 at Cambridge University, not the first great lay-writer to speak in that form: Samuel Johnson and Samuel Taylor Coleridge, among them, had offered a series of (lay) sermons.

There is also, importantly, as already noted, the introduction that Eliot penned for his edition of the *Pensées*, published in 1931. Although the passages are not directly autobiographical, they cannot be read without thinking of the writer himself. This essay may be the clearest indication we have of this pilgrim's progress toward Christianity and, in particular, Anglo-Catholicism, with its striking emphasis on the centrality of the Incarnation.

Notice this passage, to begin with, the vivid descriptions of the seventeenth-century French writer smacking of so much in Eliot's own life—and his own interests, directions, and values: Pascal, he writes, was "a man of the world among ascetics, and an ascetic among men of the world," knowing the world and having "the passion of asceticism," the differences in his case "fused into an individual whole."[4] These general characteristics both writers share, as they do the greater particulars that Eliot proceeds to delineate. Pascal's "despair, his disillusion," writes Eliot, signal no "personal weakness," but instead "are perfectly objective, because they are *essential moments in the progress of the intellectual soul*; and for the type of Pascal they are *the analogue of the drought, the dark night, which is an essential stage in the progress of the Christian mystic....*" Moreover, Pascal's was "*a despair which was a necessary prelude to, and element in, the joy of faith*" (italics added).[5] If the second quotation reminds us of *The Waste Land*, the first surely recalls *Ash-Wednesday*. Like Pascal, I surmise in any case, Eliot was "the type of one kind of religious believer, which is highly passionate and ardent, but passionate only through a powerful and regulated intellect."[6] Eliot, the poet *and* philosopher, creator *and* critic, layman of the Church of England *and* Catholic, sought to overcome needless and debilitating separation and opposition, questing to "*associate*," recognizing, as he came to do (along with Alexander Pope), productive and fecund *tension*.

The brilliant essay on Pascal reaches its thematic climax with Eliot's lengthy detailing of "the process of the mind of the intelligent believer"—note, too, the idea represented here of a "sequence" of events and understandings bringing one to the threshold of faith—*sequence* is critical, con*sequential* just as in *The Odyssey* the Trojan hero goes through a structured series of events in the Kingdom of the Dead. The tone and the texture in Eliot fairly exude the philosophical: "The Christian thinker...proceeds by rejection and elimination. He finds the world to be so and so; he finds its character inexplicable by any non-religious theory." Among religious possibilities, "he finds Christianity, and Catholic Christianity, to account most satisfactorily for the world and especially for the moral world within." Ultimately, the pilgrim "finds himself inexorably committed to the dogma of the Incarnation...." The unbeliever, on the other hand, proceeds in a quite different manner, probably, says Eliot, "with the question: Is a case of human parthenogenesis credible? and this he would call going straight to the heart of the matter."[7] Like Eliot, beginning his writing career with *observations*—his first book was the revolutionary *Prufrock and Other Observations*—the "intelligent believer" proceeds in *a posteriori* fashion, and so avoids the wrath of those like Pope who excoriate "the high Priori Road."[8] Eliot is thus subscribing to the Incarnational pattern of going in, through, and by means of.

Four Quartets is Eliot's great religious poem—or, rather, so as not to reduce or demean it, his greatest poem.[9] It is also an essay.[10] As such, it is about time, and about writing, the fifth and final section of each of the four poems taking up writing and commenting insightfully about it. Verses in *Little Gidding* echo those in *East Coker* representing rustic "daunsinge" in the Elizabethan period: for example,

> The association of man and woman
> In daunsinge, signifying matrimonie—
> A dignified and commodious sacrament.
> Two and two, necessarye coniunction,
> Holding eche other by the hand or the arm
> Which betokenth concorde.

Writing Eliot thus connects with dancing, and with matrimony, sacrament, "association," and "coniunction": "The complete consort dancing together," each word "Taking its place to support the other."

The fifth section of the first of *Four Quartets, Burnt Norton*, has carefully established both the prominence of words in the essay-poem and the nature of *the pattern* that Eliot reveals as marking time and the movement in time of words as of dance. Writing about words here, as at the end of *Little Gidding*, Eliot discusses not merely words: one thing is never (should never be) merely that one thing. By the same token, each moment burns with meaning, the past and the future alive and glowing within it. "Words move,.../ Only in time," and "Only by the form, the pattern," can they "reach / The stillness."

And so we arrive at the fifth section of the third of the *Quartets, The Dry Salvages*, where writing itself slips, slides, into time—and Eliot's most straightforward representation of and direct statement about "the pattern." The passage carries more thematic weight than any other in the entire poem, and may well be the most important lines that Eliot ever wrote. The *substance* of the observations recalls the diviners satirized in *The Waste Land* and lamented in *Ash-Wednesday*. Here, though, in *Four Quartets*, Eliot moves *through* those observations, the very things with which the "intelligent believer" always begins, to something new. He has written, of course, about the relation of time and timelessness since at least his most famous and influential essay "Tradition and the Individual Talent," included in *The Sacred Wood* (1920). "[T]o apprehend / The point of intersection of the timeless / With time, is an occupation for the saint," writes Eliot now. Most of us, though, are different: ordinary, if intelligent—no saints but, I dare say, *laymen*—and so "For most of us, there is only the unattended / Moment, the moment in and out of time." The passage seems deliberately to echo, and to call to mind and for comparison, *The Waste Land*, as well as the mythic sense of a moment in a rose (or hyacinth) garden big with promise yet fleeting, leaving one, like Keats's woeful knight in "La Belle

Dame sans Merci," wan, forlorn, and despairing. Time is the enemy for the Romantics, and Eliot faces squarely in *Four Quartets* the ever-present temptation to blame time and to attempt to leap outside it and its ravages. He offers the Christian response in terms that make Christianity and especially its critical dogma of the Incarnation a *type* of the always-sought "pattern." The lines are highly charged with meaning—just as are, Eliot says, bringing words (and writing) and theology together, time and ordinary experience.

Continuing, Eliot reveals the pattern itself: he is writing about pattern, and *sequence*, not dogma, of course: "The hint half guessed, the gift half understood, is Incarnation / Here the impossible union" occurs "Of spheres of existence," and "Here the past and future / Are conquered and reconciled...." *The* Incarnation is the becoming-man of God, in the person of Christ Jesus; it "associates" and represents the "coniunction" of immanence and transcendence. Eliot's repeated pun on "half" reveals us as guessing and understanding either one or the other—immanence or transcendence—but not both. The Incarnation is the paradigmatic instance of Incarnation—without which actual, historical event, though, we could perhaps have been saved by understanding the pattern, which Jesus revealed supremely, in every sense once and for all.

Eliot then completes *The Dry Salvages* with the following verses, which reiterate the difficulty not only of "understanding" but also of en*acting*—that is to say, embodying—that understanding, which becomes a central and critical subject in *Little Gidding*: "And right action is freedom / From past and future also," which most of us will never realize. We—laymen, perhaps—must be "content at the last / If our temporal reversion nourish / (Not too far from the yew-tree) / The life of significant soil." The idea—in still other words—that Eliot has revealed *seems* so simple, to intellection, that is. But—as my students invariably attest, and as Eliot himself suggested—such a *middle way* is of all ways the most difficult.

Perhaps—*perhaps*—that is one reason (or even *the* reason) why Eliot said what he did in the allegory that constitutes the fourth, lyrical section of *East Coker*. These five conventional, five-line, rhyming stanzas are the simplest, easiest verses in all of *Four Quartets*. Irony abounds, as the most imaginative, strictly speaking, proves most accessible to understanding, whereas the essayistic/prosaic sections, by far the most numerous, are fraught with difficulty for us. At any rate, here is the allegory of Christ, with His "sharp compassion" (and thus the uniting of apparent opposites), man's diseased state, human existence, and that Keats-like hospital, here the province and responsibility of "the dying nurse." This is no "*easie God*" (to return to Dryden). Paradox abounds, linked "sharp compassion" pointing to the pattern identified as Incarnation. Not surprisingly, then, Eliot writes, making a point on which *Four Quartets* rests: "Our only health is the disease," and so "to be restored, our sickness must grow worse," attended by the "wounded surgeon," who is Christ, and the "dying nurse." Just as a reader must ask why Eliot omitted "the" before "Incarnation," so here why is the "nurse"—evidently the Church—"dying"? One answer is obvious, and easy: look around you, and note the ever-declining membership and Church attendance. And why is that? The nature of modernity is surely to blame—partly. But is the Church, as well? You cannot but wonder that Eliot thought so—and wrote, *as a layman*, this essay-poem in response? As a supplement (in the Derridean sense of at once addition and substitution)?

Some support for a positive answer to these last questions comes from the following stanza, the opening line of which returns me (at least) to Keats's notion of "a thing of beauty" as "a joy for ever," "bind[ing] us to the earth": the earth is "our hospital," provided for by "the ruined millionaire"; if we do well, "we shall / Die of the absolute paternal care / That will not leave us, but prevents us everywhere." This reminds me also, with a certain twist, of Alexander Pope's "The Universal Prayer." Certainly, one might, and no doubt should, say that, *given Incarnation*, "The whole earth" can indeed serve as that capacity for restoration. Eliot then clarifies the way, that of the Church "a type" of the prescription hard to take but necessary and guaranteed to save: "If to be warmed, then I must freeze / And quake in frigid purgatorial fires." The prescription is harsh, severe. Is, I have to wonder, the Church dying in Eliot's view because it does not face up to these facts? (Another Anglican writer, often an apologist, the late C.H. Sisson, became convinced of it and wrote, despairingly, of his Church, introducing his own *Anglican Essays.*[11])

There *is*, I suggest, a positive connection between *Four Quartets* and the "layman's faiths" and between Eliot the devout Anglican and Dryden the "honest layman" speaking his own mind. Tradition and the individual thus come together: neither an identity nor an opposition, just as he wrote in his great essay bearing the title "Tradition and the Individual Talent." There he spoke, presciently, it turns out, of "a sense of the timeless as well as of the temporal and of the timeless and of the temporal together" as "what makes a writer traditional."[12] Their relation is complex and complicated. Eliot adds that involved "is a judgment, a comparison, in which *two things are measured by each other*" (italics added). He then proceeds to draw out the implications: "To conform merely would be for the new work not really to conform at all; it would not be new, and would therefore not be a work of art." Eliot denies that "the new is more valuable because it fits in; but its fitting in is a test of its value." Thus, concludes Eliot on this point, the work "appears to conform, and is perhaps individual, or it appears individual, and may conform; but we are *hardly likely to find that it is one and not the other*" (italics added).[13] In *Four Quartets*, I suggest, the enigmas of the "layman's faith" works find their most satisfying expression, Eliot having succeeded in working through and out the multiform complexities, fully accepting the entailed—the *embodied*—tensions.

The journey toward understanding—the pilgrim's progress—entails a way and a sequence, as Eliot himself wrote. Just as the Holy Spirit proceeds from God by means of Jesus's mediation, so does Love proceed from Being (only) through Understanding: the necessary *third*, the essential *between*, emblematic of a certain fecund tension. Understanding involves both sympathy and participation: for example, Odysseus visiting the Dead and participating in their suffering, the ancient Hebrews similarly coming "to envision the stranger's heart"[14] as a result of their captivity, their slavery, in Egypt.

Unlike earlier laymen, Eliot insists, along with Dante, that understanding entails and requires purgation. Already in *Four Quartets*, in *Burnt Norton* (1935), in fact, Eliot signals the way, pointing to the sequence dependent upon this painful detour: there simply is no direct or straight line to salvation. *The Waste Land* included "The Fire Sermon," and Eliot already recognized, with St. Augustine (and the Buddha) the value of purgation of desire, although there it seems more intellectual than earned. In *Burnt Norton*, he writes, early, of the kind of necessary "darkness to purify the soul / Emptying the sensual with deprivation / Cleansing affection from the temporal." But Oriental asceticism looms as a temptation to be resisted, no matter how attractive or how strong the pull— *Ash-Wednesday* dramatizes this "way," especially in its first two (of six) poems. Here, in "this twittering world," according to *Burnt Norton*, there is not enough darkness. The answer thus must lie in deprivation, not to be identified as or equated with simple emptying. Little wonder, then, that Eliot defines salvation as the labor of the saint. Since the spirit seduces and the fancy is a deceitful will-of-the-wisp, attention is crucial, along with discipline and distinction. Indeed, as Eliot writes in *East Coker*, men and women find ourselves, ironically enough, in a Dantesque situation and condition, here in this would-be modern "purgatorio": "In the middle, not only in the middle of the way / But all the way, in a dark wood," in fact, "On the edge of a grimpen," without security and "menaced by monsters, fancy lights, / Risking enchantment." And old men and their supposed wisdom? Eliot will have none of it. Let me hear, instead, he writes, of "their folly": "Their fear of fear and frenzy, their fear of possession, / Of belonging to another, or to others, or to God." For, after all, he concludes, "The only wisdom we can hope to acquire / Is the wisdom of humility: humility is endless." A necessary reminder, no doubt, to the layman, to the individual(ist).

Just before the lyrical fourth section of this poem, *East Coker*, Eliot writes, his lines smacking of the essayistic, always conscious, himself, of the difficulty of writing (this, here), always "in the moment," as it were: "You say I am repeating / Something I have said before. I shall say it again. / Shall I say it again?" What follows is a series of paradoxies worthy of the great essayist G.K. Chesterton, author of—inter alia— *Orthodoxy*, who once averred that you know nothing until you know nothing.

Little Gidding insists on acting, on taking action. It is as if, having offered the critical declaration in *The Dry Salvages* that "The hint half guessed, the gift half understood, is Incarnation," Eliot now moves to the con*sequences* of that recognition and acceptance. Idea is not enough—not even the Logos; embodiment is necessary, and for us forked creatures it has to follow the Word.

The poem starts off by deliberately recalling *The Waste Land*: "April is the cruelest month" becomes here "Midwinter spring is its own season." Not only is the sensibility changed, but also the texture. More: "This is the spring time / But not in time's covenant." May gives way to "may time," a term that Eliot used previously in *Ash-Wednesday*. "You" are imagined as on the way to the significant, ruined chapel erected by Nicholas Ferrar at Little Gidding, the place where King Charles I stopped and prayed, following his defeat at Naseby in 1642, seven years before his beheading by Cromwell's Puritan hordes. Eliot invokes "a broken king" and the birth of Jesus, directing "you" to "turn behind the pig-sty to the dull façade / And the tombstone." Expectation is the issue, surprise, difference, and serendipity. The place is special, special in part as a "type." The moment passing, as in the proverbial rose garden, is here, now, and everywhere. If you came this way, writes Eliot, again saying it again, you would need to relinquish "Sense and notion," for you are here not to "verify," "Instruct yourself," or satisfy curiosity, but, simply, "to kneel." Here, "prayer has been valid": *valid* prayer, rather than the familiar "effective." The point is worship: Worship is All.

The most important *event* in *Four Quartets* is surely the encounter with the "familiar compound ghost" in *Little Gidding*, a figure clearly designed to recall Tiresias, whom Eliot calls "the most important personage" in *The Waste Land*. The passage smacks of Odysseus's climactic voyage to the Kingdom of the Dead, where he is instructed by Tiresias and learns much from other ghosts as he encounters nothingness and death. The encounter in *Little Gidding* occurs, significantly, in the dawning light, on the streets of bombed-out London, where the poet patrols as fire warden—a modern kingdom of the dead (and the dying). The passage is highly charged, mimicking its occasion: "the dark dove with the flickering tongue / Had passed below the horizon of his homing / While the dead leaves still rattled on like tin." Here, now, "Between three districts whence the smoke arose / I met one walking, loitering and hurried...." The verses grab, hold, disturb, almost disembowel you. The "dark dove" prepares for the later representation (Section 4) of the dove as Holy Spirit, "three" again captures the attention, and the paradox of "loitering and hurried" strikes by-now-familiar chords, preparing for the introduction of the *compound* figure. Eliot's interests from at least *The Waste Land* forward are met here at the break of day—there may even be a hint or two of Prufrock ("Let us go then, you and I, . . ."): the both/ands recall the representation of the mediating "Lady" of *Ash-Wednesday*, here "Both intimate and unfamiliar." The speaker immediately assumes "a double part," and in turn hears "another's voice cry: 'What! are *you* here?' / Although we were not. I was still the same, / Knowing myself yet being someone other." The words become even more resonant and pregnant with meaning and significance: "Too strange to each other for misunderstanding, / In concord at this intersection time / Of meeting nowhere, no before and after, / We trod the pavement in a dead patrol." "Concord" and "intersection" echo and foreshadow at the same time. All seems less like a *Walpurgisnacht* or phantasmagoria than the conditions for understanding: the self has an ek-static moment, looking at itself while looking outside itself, a strangeness strangely effected by this "familiar" figure who is yet "strange" enough to prevent misunderstanding. Eliot clearly complicates relations, effecting them—dramatizing how they come about. While each moment burns with meaning, this encounter stands as a paradigmatic moment, mimicking the relation of *the Incarnation* and Incarnation.

Now the poet speaks for the first time to the ghost, who in ways resembles an older and wiser Prufrock, and as he speaks, the poet comes across like Wordsworth engaging the leech-gatherer in "Resolution and Independence": not just uncomprehending but initially self-absorbed and pointedly not understanding at the most basic level of comprehension, insouciant, cloddish. The ghost responds, curtly, "I am not eager to rehearse / My thoughts and theory which you have forgotten." In any case, he adds, emphatically, "These things have served their purpose: let them be." He then urges the speaker "to forgive / Both bad and good."

The following message is professorial, magisterial actually—and no doubt surprising in its abruptness, its intensity, its moral compulsion. This is action—in action and urgent. We move from the earlier stress on spring and "may time" to autumn, harvest, and reaping—but will it be Keatsian in a melancholic embrace? Even "last year's words belong to last year's language / And next year's words await another voice." The issue involves, obviously, past and future, recalling again "Tradition and the Individual Talent" and reverberating with *Hamlet* and the notorious ghost of Old Hamlet as well as with the Homeric tale of Elpenor, abandoned for a while by Odysseus. The ghost describes his spirit as "unappeased and peregrine," walking "Between two worlds become much like each other." He is surprised to "find words," but since "our concern was speech, and speech impelled us / To purify the dialect of the tribe," then he will, rather unpropitiously, "disclose the gifts reserved for age / To set a crown upon your lifetime's effort." The tone has thus turned, the ghost intent upon teaching by disabusing, by scaling back expectations, and upon bringing about some humility. There is, he says, beginning his enumeration of three points,

> First, the cold friction of expiring sense
> Without enchantment, offering no promise
>   But bitter tastelessness of shadow fruit
>   As body and soul begin to fall asunder.
> Second, the conscious impotence of rage
>   At human folly, and the laceration
>   Of laughter at what ceases to amuse.
> And last, the rending pain of re-enactment
>   Of all that you have done, and been; the shame
>   Of motives late revealed, and the awareness
> Of things ill done and done to others' harm
>   Which once you took for exercise of virtue.
>   Then fools' approval stings, and honour stains.

So the "exasperated spirit," the ghost asserts, "Proceeds, unless restored by that refining fire," which he defines, recalling the passage of dancing in *East Coker*, as "Where you must move in measure, like a dancer." It is as close, I believe, to a confession as Eliot ever offered in print. The end contains hope, though not promise. The ghost "faded on the blowing of the horn" (not, as in *Hamlet*, the crowing of the cock).

The next section of *Little Gidding*, the third, consists of two crucial, related parts. The first is statement-al, the second quite different in tone and texture. Together, they represent the effects of what has just been described, as close perhaps as one can come in the modern world to a conversation with the dead. It is as if the poet's world has been rocked, emotionally, viscerally. We have seen and heard the intellectualizing, but until now we have not experienced *the effects* on him of that thought. Understanding is not, in other words, complete— not until purgation occurs and participation follows.

Section 3 of *Little Gidding* thus opens with reiteration of the mighty "three" and proceeds to the poems' clearest definition of (true) love, a *sophia* close to *agape*. The whole verse paragraph carries the feel of summary *cum* clarification with definition—as in Dryden's *Religio Laici*, neither extreme works, but then such indifference as *The Waste Land* reveals, and satirizes, is no workable answer either: three conditions "look alike," although they "differ completely." These are "Attachment to self and to things and to persons; detachment / From self and from things and from persons; and, growing between them, indifference / Which resembles the others as death resembles life." As to "the use of memory," it is for "liberation—not less of love but expanding / Of love beyond desire," and that, if accomplished, brings about "liberation / From the future as well as the past." In any case, "The faces and places vanish," along with "the self which, as it could, loved them, / To become renewed, transfigured, in another pattern." Here, then, at last, past and future are figured, as well as desire—our notable enemies. The answer to them resembles Pope's representation of expanding love at the close of *An Essay on Man*: the expanding of love *beyond desire*, the pattern Incarnational.

The speaker does, indeed, seem transfigured as he writes of the inevitability of sin, quoting the medieval mystic Dame Julian of Norwich and acknowledging (while thus embodying) participation: neither he nor anyone else, despite efforts and claims, is or can ever be without sin. The opening verse indicates by its structure that sin's inevitability does not tell the whole story, or afford license: "Sin is Behovely, but /All shall be well, and /All manner of thing shall be well." Striking now is the "I" who speaks directly (if not exactly openly); Eliot enacts lessons delivered and urged by the "familiar compound ghost." He has learned; more, he now understands. Paradoxically, the new prominence of the "I" emerges with the recognition of participation (even with John Milton), of the importance of the "complete consort" working together and supporting each other. The (new) tone engages. The speaker may think of people "not wholly commendable," immersed in strife, but rather than respond reciprocally, he concludes, pacifically, "We cannot revive old factions / We cannot restore old policies/ Or follow an antique drum."

The recognition seems hard-earned, if compatible with observations made more than two decades earlier in "Tradition and the Individual Talent." All those who oppose and those opposed "are folded in a single party": so much for sectarian differences and hatreds. Left us who survive is "a symbol: / A symbol perfected in death." The speaker's words move from such recognition to the faith and proclamation that, *in any case*, "All manner of thing shall be well / By the purification of the motive / In the ground of our beseeching." Ground revealed carries the power to purify.

The fourth, lyrical section of *Little Gidding* amplifies the points just made, extending the autobiographical understanding and (further) generalizing it. Just about everything is here; just about everything comes together here—in this one statement.

> The dove descending breaks the air
> With flame of incandescent terror
> Of which the tongues declare
> The discharge from sin and error.
> The only hope, or else despair
>   Lies in the choice of pyre or pyre—
>   To be redeemed from fire by fire.

The fire of purgation and purification redeems the fire of desire and lust and greed and gluttony and so much more. Love proceeds from and depends fully upon Understanding. Love, in fact, "devised the torment," is "the unfamiliar Name / Behind the hands that wove / The intolerable shirt of flame" before which "human power" is powerless. Our choice is, simply, to be "Consumed by either fire or fire."

What remains, is the fifth section, already discussed. What is now to be emphasized, has not, however, been observed. I mean that the longish first verse paragraph treats writing, a subject, as I have previously noted, of each of the poems comprising *Four Quartets*. In *Little Gidding* the question demands consideration if not answer: in a poem about time and timelessness, desire and love, pattern(s) and Incarnation, why so much attention to writing? Why, in fact, writing at all as a subtopic in such an essay-poem?

The initial, simple response is that writing, as here represented, partakes of that pattern that Eliot has critically revealed; it, too, in other words, is a *type*: Eliot confirms the point immediately after describing writing and calling "Every poem an epitaph": "And any action / Is a step to the block, to the fire, down the sea's throat / Or to an illegible stone: and that is where we start." Moreover, adds Eliot in the final verse paragraph: "We shall not cease from exploration / And the end of all our exploring / Will be to arrive where we started / And know the place for the first time." It is, he insists, "A condition of complete simplicity"—at the same time "Costing not less than everything." The faith is based in certainty that accepts the inclusion of doubt: "And all shall be well and / All manner of thing shall be well," the repetition and placement of the conjunction signaling continuity.

From these final words of *Four Quartets* I return to those following the account of words earlier in the fifth section of *Little Gidding*, words as enigmatic as any that Eliot ever wrote: "We die with the dying," Eliot declares; "See, they depart, and we go with them." The "dead" and the "dying" inhabit perhaps different dimensions. The difference, in any case, returns us to those quoted earlier: "but that which is only living / Can only die," words that are followed immediately by the declaration that "Only by the form, the pattern, / Can words or music reach / The stillness...." The subject is, as it has to be, death, and dying, and living on: "the co-existence," and so "the end and the beginning were always there / Before the beginning and after the end. / And all is always now." Has anyone, ever, come closer to representing Resurrection? Or to confirming that, while the spirit kills, the letter gives life? The job of the poet is, then, endless: "restoring / With a new verse the ancient rhyme"—his or her work as layperson critical.

6

"Religious feeling without religious images": E.B. White's Essays and the Poetics of Participation

The great familiar essayist Elwyn Brooks ("Andy") White, *New Yorker* writer, author of *Stuart Little* and *Charlotte's Web*, one of the most agreeable prose masters in English, one of the most engaging and sympathetic makers of story fictional and nonfictional, participated in, embodying, what he ascribes to his mentor Henry David Thoreau a century earlier: he too renders "religious feeling without religious images."[1] The feelings are there, the ideas too, but absent are the familiar and conventional religious images, doctrine, and dogma.

"A Slight Sound at Evening," written as a centenary tribute to *Walden* and its maker, is a striking case in point. White has said that "steadiness" lies at "the heart" of the great book, which he goes on to define in the following words:

> —confidence, faith, the discipline of looking always at what is to be seen, undeviating gratitude for the life-everlasting that he found growing in his front yard. "There is nowhere recorded a simple and irrepressible satisfaction with the gift of life, any memorable praise of God." He worked to correct that deficiency. *Walden* is his acknowledgment of the gift of life.... (236)

The terms are rich, religious, and profound. As much as he admired Henry Thoreau, White did not share his Transcendentalism, as may already be apparent in the words that I have quoted. White evidently subscribed to some notion of God, and, though not a believer in pantheism, he most certainly raised paean after paean to the immanence of a mysterious power in the universe.

In the terms above, White raises an insistent question. "Religious feeling without religious images" itself images, perfectly, a recurring and fundamental pattern in man's quest as human in relation to some putative Divine. In brief, here represented is the preeminent post-Reformation issue for the newly freed, newly enfranchised layperson, now able to read Scripture for himself or herself. Translated into the largest, and ultimate, terms, the issue becomes that of which reading is a part, albeit a particularly important and striking one: what is, exactly, the layman's relation (and responsibility) to religious institutions, more specifically, to established Christian institutions, one of which is, of course, the Church? Within that all-encompassing question, and depending on the particular interests and directions of an individual, how does one deal with the plaguing matter of exclusivism? That is to say, can human being stomach the at least implicit claim, even of the institution that calls itself, and claims to be, *Catholic* and therefore universal, that only those baptized in the faith are to achieve eternal salvation? What, in short, of those born before Christ lived as God Incarnate and became *the Way*, outside and beyond which no one can expect to enjoy the rewards and the joys of Heaven? In a word, the question is universalism— which accounts for the advent and rise of Deism. In his *Religio Laici or A Laymans Faith* (1682), John Dryden put it with characteristic succinctness and clarity: the imagined Deist "urges," "No *Supernatural Worship* can be *True*: / Because a *general Law* is that alone / Which must to *all*, and every *where* be known" (169–71).[2] Dryden then acknowledges the power and force of the argument, referring ultimately to God's Nature, His Love, and His Charity:

> Of all Objections this indeed is chief
> To startle Reason, stagger frail Belief:
> We grant, 'tis true, that Heav'n from humane Sense

Has hid the secret paths of *Providence*:
But *boundless Wisdom, boundless Mercy*, may
Find ev'n for those *be-wildred* Souls, a *way*:
If from his *Nature Foes* may Pity claim,
Much more may *Strangers* who ne'er heard his *Name*.
And though *no Name* be for *Salvation* known,
But that of his *Eternal Sons* alone;
Who knows how far transcending Goodness can
Extend the *Merits* of *that Son* to *Man*?
Who knows what *Reasons* may his *Mercy* lead;
Or *Ignorance invincible* may plead? (284–97)

The great French writer of the first half of the twentieth century, Simone Weil, proffered an answer to the Deist's staggering objection. Born a Jew, Weil experienced a direct encounter with Christ. This was in late 1938, as she was reciting, as she often did, the seventeenth-century English poet George Herbert's "Love": "le Christ lui-meme est descendu et m'a prise."[3] The experience changed her life; although she was never baptized, never sought communion in the (Roman Catholic) Church, Weil became a major proponent of Christianity and a frequent, strong, and effective advocate of and apologist for Christianity. Unorthodox as it certainly is, Weil's essential argument is, in the words of one of her most astute critics, that "Christianity had existed before the incarnation of Christ."[4] This she pursues in, for example, a series of brilliantly imaginative and controversial readings of famous Greek works, notably *Antigone, The Iliad, Prometheus Bound*, and *Electra*. Indeed, she "reads myth from a Christian perspective,"[5] differing thus from "demythologizers" like Rudolf Bultmann.

Still and all, a nonbaptized person offering apologias for Christianity? Here, I find myself in a somewhat similar position, for, although I am baptized, once and for a long while was a member of the Southern Baptist Church, until I "moved my letter" to the Congregational Church (officially, the United Church of Christ), I very rarely attend services. More, I find both those churches doctrinally, intellectually, and emotionally alien. My sympathies lie with (T.S. Eliot's and Dryden's)

Anglo-Catholicism—although I have yet to begin steps to convert or to be received into the Church of England. Weil thought her position, at least, advantageous to apologetics despite the vulnerability thus created for herself.

Weil's essential (Christological) understanding appears in bold relief in such a statement as the following, in her book *Intimations of Christianity among the Ancient Greeks*:

> Human thought and the universe constitute the books of revelation *par excellence*, if the attention lighted by love and faith, knows to decipher them. The reading of them is a proof, and indeed the only certain proof. After having read the *Iliad* in Greek, no one would dream of wondering whether the professor who taught him the Greek alphabet had deceived him.[6]

The Catholic Church, though, according to Weil, "fails to fulfil its call to universality."[7]

With Weil's extremely suggestive and provocative thesis, I wish to juxtapose T.S. Eliot's take on the Christian pattern of Incarnation prior to his conversion to what he himself described as Anglo-Catholicism. Such understanding is available to a reading that proceeds from, and is bred by (to use his mentor Dryden's term), the major revelation he writes of in *The Dry Salvages*: "The hint half guessed, the gift half understood, is Incarnation."[8] By omitting the definite article before the term "Incarnation," Eliot signals, as we have observed, the universal, timeless pattern of which *the* Incarnation stands as paradigm. It is as simple and yet as difficult as that: "A condition of complete simplicity / (Costing not less than everything)" (*Little Gidding*).[9]

Here is Eliot, writing in *The Sacred Wood*, some seven years before his conversion—the passage occurs in the long second chapter of that book, "Imperfect Critics," specifically in a section titled "A Romantic Aristocrat": "Romanticism is a short cut to the strangeness without the reality, and it leads its disciples only back upon themselves."[10] Eliot was, of course, an inveterate baiter of Romantics and offered an alternative to Wordsworth's conceptions of both poetry and the poet in his most famous and influential essay "Tradition and the Individual Talent," also included in *The Sacred Wood*. Notice carefully Eliot's sentence: he objects here to directness, to the attempt, in Romanticism, to circumvent—to short-circuit and skip over, in fact—one stage or step or point in favor of a quick and efficient apprehension of that which is desired. The pattern is, thus, exactly, that of Incarnation as revealed in *the* Incarnation: there is no direct way, only the mediated way, of proceeding *in, through, and by means of* the "inferior" term. You approach God (only) through the Person of Christ Jesus; you reach some desired strangeness only through reality. Reality comes first, and you never can completely transcend that primal stage.

On such an understanding, you grasp the universality and the timelessness of essential pattern, always everywhere already present in the world. It is there, for example, in the Greeks, as Simone Weil postulated. Take *The Odyssey*, especially its climactic twelfth book, in which the Trojan hero voyages to the Underworld—"The Kingdom of the Dead"—to consult with the prophet Tiresias. There Odysseus becomes purged—or, rather, begins his journey toward understanding. Encountering nothingness, the inescapable fact of death, his participation in its inevitability, thus his equal share in human-ness, Odysseus emerges as a changed man, no longer so reckless and self-centered, more generous, more sympathetic, and newly self-controlled. As Dante would later show in *The Divine Comedy*, the way to Paradise (as back to Ithaca and the waiting arms of Odysseus's ever-faithful wife Penelopeia and son Telemachus) leads in, through, and by means of detour to Purgatorio. There is no escaping the difficulty, in spite of the Romantics (such as James Joyce's Stephen Dedalus, determined to escape the maze, forgo the Roman Catholic priesthood, and approach God directly).

Religious feeling without religious images?

I submit that Eliot's "way" is preferable to Weil's, for all the latter's attractiveness, and indeed similarity. *Incarnation* allows for—in fact, defines—timelessness and universality: the pattern is built into the very nature of things human and otherwise and is available, and has always been, everywhere and to all persons. Christian revelation represents that pattern at its clearest, in every sense *embodying* it and making it so clear that it should be neither missed nor misunderstood (although, given the Fall and consequent human will-fulness, it has been, continues to be, and will forever remain so).

In Incarnation, understood in Eliot's terms, I read a Catholicity—a pointed non-sectarianism—perhaps still lurking even in Weil. Maybe I diminish Weil's understanding, for she certainly sought universality. At any rate, Eliot's understanding is clear, detailed, and reasonable. Pay careful attention, too, to his tone when, in writing of Pascal, he describes "the process of the mind of the intelligent believer," the passage autobiographical in the only way that Eliot knew or would permit, and that is indirectly. He is here, as a matter of fact, explicitly distinguishing between the apologist (of whom Weil was one) and "the Christian thinker" defined as "the man who is trying consciously and conscientiously to explain to himself the sequence which culminates in faith." The apologist, on the other hand, writes Eliot, "proceeds by rejection and elimination." Eliot has in mind, differently, the ordinary layman, like himself, like me, like you perhaps. Then these important words:

> [The intelligent believer, the pilgrim] finds the world to be so and so; he finds its character inexplicable by any non-religious theory: among religions he finds Christianity, and Catholic Christianity, to account most satisfactorily for the world and especially for the moral world within; and thus, by what [Cardinal John Henry] Newman calls "powerful and concurrent" reasons, he finds himself inexorably committed to the dogma of the Incarnation.[11]

Eliot's argument is thus itself Incarnational in structure and pattern, embodying the doctrine, showing the way.

Eliot, I think, satisfactorily accounts for universality and timelessness. "Pattern" cuts to the heart of the issue, providing both specificity and clarity and offering explanations that his own procedures both support and affirm. White's description of Henry Thoreau—by no means Christian in *his* understanding, being a confirmed Transcendentalist and pur-itan—taps into this same idea, while hardly identifying with it: "religious feeling without religious images" points, I believe, to the possibility of participation and so of shared understanding across doctrinal, dogmatic, institutional, and intellectual differences of great breadth.

As to White, I have written elsewhere about his way of "embodying truth," for example, in "Death of a Pig."[12] I shall not repeat my arguments here, only mention that, as is common with the familiar form of the essay, in which White works and of which he is a master craftsman, the essayistic character bears responsibility for carrying the burden of meaning: he it is, after all, who has undergone experience and tried and weighed it for meaning. I want to take a new tack in treating White, and that is to focus on his "poetics of participation," another aspect of his offering "religious feeling without religious images."

Understanding is the name of the game, the best one in town. We read (texts) in order to understand them; we want to understand them, not so as to understand understanding (as Geoffrey Hartman supposes), but so that we understand what they understand. Understanding, willy-nilly, involves participation, as participation involves sympathy. I can no more understand a text by standing outside it than I can hope to understand the world by withdrawing and absenting myself from it, its challenges, opportunities, horrors, and glories. The ancient Hebrews learned to "envision the stranger's heart" thanks to their bondage in Egypt.[13] Odysseus comes to self-control, sympathy, and generosity through his visit to the Kingdom of the Dead, where he participates in nothingness. The Logos understands man because He took our form and being in the Person of His Son, Christ Jesus, thus making love possible as He so loved us.

We like people who understand, who are understanding. E.B. White is one of those writers who is understanding—of the human predicament, of our capacity for both meanness and greatness, of time's apparently merciless march, of his own failings and penchant for error. "Andy" White seems to be one of the most understanding persons we know. He also appears notoriously understandable, in his own right. Too rarely do we go further and ask and seek to understand what lay behind that capacity for understanding: his own understanding.

Possibly a paradox: sometimes at least, participation entails keeping quiet, holding your peace, controlling the urge and tendency to speak. Nowhere is this truer than in teaching, which includes a pastoral function. In conversation, too, with a friend or acquaintance, or when solicited for advice, or in reading, listening can mean participating.

I begin, not with White, but with his fellow familiar essayist, surgeon-teacher-writer Richard Selzer. No one I know has more effectively dramatized what I call "the poetics of participation," not even Andy White. In his brilliant essay "A Worm from My Notebook," Selzer tells the story of a poor Zairean farmer named Ibrahim who contracts the lethal Guinea worm. Selzer precedes the fiction with incisive commentary about writing and writing this story. By means of the obvious echo of parasite and host, the story itself dramatizes the worm's literal participation in the man. Just as, moreover, dreaded *Dracunculus medinensis* "worms" its way inside, so does the story "worm" its way into the reader—but then the reader also "worms" her or his way into the story. Selzer has alerted us to these goings-on in inviting us to participate in the *writing* of the story. After all, he writes, you have to love your characters, and the reader must participate in that love.

> Shall we write the story together? A Romance of Parasitology? Let me tell you how it goes thus far. I will give you a peek into my notebook where you will see me struggling to set words down on a blank piece of paper. At first whimsically, capriciously, even insincerely. Later, in dead earnest. You will see at precisely what moment the writer ceases to think of his character as an instrument to be manipulated and think of him as

someone with whom he has fallen in love. For it is always, must always be, a matter of love.[14]

No one, perhaps, has ever written better about writing. Here, the poetics of participation becomes, inevitably, the ethics and even the theology of participation.

Now listen to White, starting off his foreword to the 1977 collected *Essays*: his apologia for essaying and an enduring, sustaining description of such a writer's work. His opening words, the beginning paragraph, are these well-chosen few:

> The essayist is a self-liberated man, sustained by the childish belief that everything he thinks about, everything that happens to him, is of general interest. He is a fellow who thoroughly enjoys his work, just as people who take bird walks enjoy theirs. Each new excursion of the essayist, each new "attempt," differs from the last and takes him into new country. This delights him. Only a person who is congenitally self-centered has the effrontery and the stamina to write essays. (vii)

The last sentence here often receives more attention and is assumed to bear more weight than it deserves in context. It participates—dare I say?—in a whole that does not so much compromise it, or is compromised by it, as it qualifies it. In truth, the last sentence springs a certain surprise, even with "self-liberated" in the first words of this *"Gen'rous Converse"* (Alexander Pope, *An Essay on Criticism*); it stings—rather than packs a wallop—alerting the reader to the necessity to *read*.

White's assumption emerges clearly: the essayist believes that his or her reader will show interest in his every word, thought, saunter, discovery. The reason is—or at least, *a* reason is—that the reader matches the writer, the essayist, in *giving herself up to* the other, in participating in adventure, in following "the course of interpretive discovery" (Paul H. Fry).[15] A pattern exists, in other words, in which reader and writer alike participate. That White immediately, still in only his second sentence here, turns to metaphor confirms the point, metaphor being the agent of reciprocity, says Cynthia Ozick. The word "excursion" at the beginning of the next sentence bolsters the sense White develops, whether consciously or not: "excursion" echoes—in the ear of the participating reader—with "excursus," *linking* walking and writing. The essay is, as everyone knows, a famously peripatetic and ambulatory form, the essayist frequently out walking and almost as frequently writing about his walks (Thoreau, William Hazlitt, Edward Hoagland, Sam Pickering, to take but a few who spring immediately to mind); essaying is, in fact, a kind of walking about, a sauntering, "taking a line out for a walk" (Joseph Epstein, drawing on the artist Paul Klee).[16] Walking is a metaphor for essaying. By extension, then, we come to see that—and how—writing and living life participate in one another and engage in fruitful reciprocity.

In the writing that follows in this charming, engaging, and insightful book, the *Essays*, made of 31 essays divided into 7 sections, White dons the mantle of Michel de Montaigne, acknowledged father of the essay. He may feel free, this "self-liberated man," to "pull on any sort of shirt, be any sort of person, according to his mood or his subject matter—philosopher, scold, jester, raconteur, confidant, pundit, devil's advocate, enthusiast" (vii), and yet there stands, steadfast, the form, bequeathed to him (and us) by the sixteenth-century Frenchman. Nobody has been able to define it, few to describe it accurately; no one comes closer than White, pointing to its tension, its way of bringing together seeming opposites:

> even the essayist's escape from discipline is only a partial escape: the essay, although a relaxed form, imposes its own disciplines, raises its own problems, and these disciplines and problems soon become apparent and (we all hope) act as a deterrent to anyone wielding a pen merely because he entertains random thoughts or is in a happy or *wandering* mood. (viii; italics added)

White has even written, a few sentences before, of "the essay form (or lack of form)" (vii). Rather than contradiction,

I suggest, rather even than complication, White reveals inclusion. Everywhere, the form (or lack of form) that he embraces and celebrates opposes, and resists, exclusion, making room, inviting in—"to life's dance" (235). I take White's apt phrase from "A Slight Sound at Evening," an essay commemorating the centennial of Henry Thoreau's *Walden*. White's following words are pregnant with meaning and significance:

> ...the book is like an invitation to life's dance, assuring the troubled recipient that no matter what befalls him in the way of success or failure he will always be welcome at the party— that the music is played for him, too, if he will but listen and move his feet. (235)

Invited to participate, the "recipient"—including reader— need but do so, avers White.

White himself, of course, accepts the invitation to participate in "life's dance," finding—if not quite contentment— enjoyment and satisfactions in country life, obviously in writing, in the old Ford Model-T, the sights and sounds of New York City, a young girl rehearsing bare-back for the John Ringling North circus. He *is* "a fellow who thoroughly enjoys his work," and a note of affirmativeness marks his essays, as it does, says Joseph Epstein, the work of all major writers in the essay form.

In writing about Thoreau, that "regular hair-shirt of a man" (241), "a sort of Nature Boy" (234), whose greatest work "is his acknowledgment of the gift of life" (236), White shows us that literary commentary involves fundamentally active participation in the work being read. White's is thus no cool, detached, distanced, or simply professional "approach"; instead, he seems almost flooded by *Walden*. White even writes in a place resembling that famous cabin two miles from Concord at a clearing near Walden Pond. Notice the distinct and specific echoes of Thoreau in this confessional paragraph, words and phrases not so much taken from the Transcendentalist as shared with him—White has accepted the invitation and now, responding, dances with Thoreau, with whom he does not, however, simply identify:

> As for me, I cannot in this short ramble give a simple and sincere account of my own life, but I think Thoreau might find it instructive to know that this memorial essay is being written in a house that, through no intent on my part, is the same size and shape as his own domicile on the pond—about ten by fifteen, tight, plainly finished, and at a little distance from my Concord. The house in which I sit this morning was built to accommodate a boat, not a man, but by long experience I have learned that in most respects it shelters me better than the larger dwelling where my bed is, and which, by design, is a manhouse not a boathouse. Here in the boathouse I am a wilder and, it would appear, a healthier man, by a safe margin. I have a chair, a bench, a table, and I can walk into the water if I tire of the land. My house fronts a cove. Two fishermen have just arrived to spot fish from the air—an osprey and a man in a small yellow plane who works for the fish company. The man, I have noticed, is less well equipped than the hawk, who can dive directly on his fish and carry it away without telephoning. A mouse and a squirrel share the house with me. The building is, in fact, a multiple dwelling, a *semidetached* affair. It is because I am *semidetached* while here that I find it possible to transact this private business with the fewest obstacles. (237; italics added)

Participation, not identification. The fisherman in the plane, moreover, lacks the hawk's success, for the latter dives in with the fish. White, differently, shares his house, which he also shares with his mentor Henry David Thoreau.

A few pages later, following added white space, White acknowledges that he "sometimes amuse[s himself] by bringing Henry Thoreau back to life and showing him the sights" (240). Thoreau thus now shares scenes and experiences with the later writer and admirer, participating with *him*, timelessness also intersecting time here. White imagines Thoreau's responses and allows his words to mix with his own. White then moves to conclusion with a striking paragraph about the exact nature of the relationship between the earlier writer and himself, the reader of and commentator on the former—no solitary walking for White:

> At any rate, I'd like to stroll about the countryside in Thoreau's company for a day, observing the modern scene, inspecting today's snowstorm, pointing out the sights, and offering belated apologies for my sins. Thoreau is unique among writers in that those who admire him find him uncomfortable to live with—a regular hairshirt of a man....I should hate to be called a Thoreavian, yet I wince every time I walk into the barn I'm pushing before me, seventy-five feet by forty, and the author of *Walden* has served as my conscience through the long stretches of my trivial days. (241)

Here, whether intentionally or not, White reveals his difference from Thoreau, who, in my judgment at least, is pointedly uninviting and always seeming above us ordinary folks. I for one find him unwilling to participate in our lives.

And yet—White solicits Thoreau's companionship. He ends this brilliant tribute, this sterling example of familiar criticism, with this properly compromised paragraph:

> Hairshirt or no, he is a better companion than most, and I would not swap him for a soberer or more reasonable friend even if I could. I can reread his famous invitation with undiminished excitement. The sad thing is that not more acceptances have been received, that so many decline for one reason or another, pleading some previous engagement or ill health. But the invitation stands. It will beckon as long as this remarkable book stays in print—which will be as long as there are August afternoons in the intervals of a gentle rainstorm, as long as there are ears to catch the faint sounds of the orchestra. I find it agreeable to sit here this morning, in a house of correct proportions, and hear across a century of time his flute, his frogs, and his seductive summons to the wildest revels of them all. (241–42)

White thus invites us to join *him* and with him in experiencing a writer said to invite us to "life's dance"—one who never invited us to join him in dancing or in sharing another's

writing. White is an altogether more agreeable person—
because he is so understanding.

Perhaps nowhere in the essays does White show greater
understanding and compassion than in the justly celebrated
"Death of a Pig," with its deftness of touch and supreme rhetorical control of a situation named as "murder" and treated
with humor.[17] The critic has, in turn, to be careful, and wary,
and try for similar deftness and delicacy of touch in writing of
this comic piece, this humorous essay. As often, White here
represents the situation as embodying a pattern, in which he
comes to participate and so to understand (similarly in "Once
More to the Lake," repetition of the father in the son signals
participation in time): "The scheme of buying a spring pig in
blossom-time, feeding it through summer and fall, and butch-
ering it when the solid cold weather arrives, is a familiar scheme
to me and follows an antique pattern" (17). Unfortunately for
pig and man in this case, "The classic outline of the tragedy
was lost," and as a result White now adds, he "found [him]self
cast suddenly in the role of pig's friend and physician—a farci-
cal character with an enema bag for a prop. I had a presenti-
ment, the very first afternoon, that the play would never regain
its balance and that my sympathies were now wholly with the
pig" (ibid.). The nature of the play being performed may have
changed—from tragedy to farce and "slapstick"—but White
has a role to play, and he participates fully.

The trouble is, White "wanted no interruption in the regu-
larity of feeding, the steadiness of growth, the even succession
of days. I wanted no interruption,...no deviation" (18). He
thinks, in other words, at the outset of his troubles, of *his* troubles, of himself, and an expected and comforting routine. Like
the dying pig, White needs to be purged. Ironically, his comes
as a result of administering an enema to the suffering animal,
an intimate participation. "I discovered," he writes, that "the
pig's lot and mine were inextricably bound now....His suffering soon became the embodiment of all earthly wretchedness"
(21). Thus White participates in the pig's lot. In so doing, and
still very much self-centered, he "knew that what could be true

of my pig could be true also of the rest of my tidy world" (22).
Still, not only does White hold his pig "steadily in the bowl of
[his] mind," but he also shares (in) his pain and suffering, the
point accented by White's use of a phrase recalling the vet's
diagnosis: but whereas the latter spoke of "deep hemorrhagic
infarcts" (21), White writes that he eventually "cried internal-
ly—deep hemorrhagic intears" (23). Sympathy, in other words,
and participation, but not identification.

White writes here, he says, because someone needs to "do
the accounting" (17). He needed, apparently, to share the
story, perhaps thereby, via confession, to assuage (at least) his
felt guilt. After all, "the premature expiration of a pig is, I
soon discovered,...a sorrow in which [the community] feels
fully involved. I have written this account," he continues, in
the last paragraph, "in penitence and in grief, as a man who
failed to raise his pig, and to explain my deviation from the
classic course of so many raised pigs" (24).

Here Is New York is surely one of White's most revered and
most successful essays (for us post-"9/11" readers it contains
eery and horrid anticipations and predictions of airplanes
plowing into towers and skyscrapers). It first appeared in
Holiday magazine and was later reprinted as a small book.[18] In
the foreword to *Essays* White himself finds that it has "been
seriously affected by the passage of time and now stand[s] as
[one of the] period pieces: I wrote it in the summer of 1948,
during a hot spell. The city I described has disappeared, and
another city has emerged in its place—one that I'm not familiar with" (viii). So saying, he accomplishes more than one
important thing: he affirms the timeliness of time and its crucial thematic place throughout his writing, and he confirms
the critical role of familiarity, in writing as in life, a subject
directly focused in, for instance, "Home-Coming," about a
very different kind of home. That White names familiarity as
key to understanding in New York and Maine alike, despite
their massive differences, is precisely the point: they share
something, you find something crucial repeated, and a pattern
emerges and persists.

Pattern, borne of repetition and its understanding the prod-uct of observation, points *Here Is New York*. White's method and procedure, though, are subtle, his manner deliberate but delicate. Take this passage of keen observation that breeds less a pattern than a difference enriched by the reader's perception of the echo of T.S. Eliot's Tiresias, that "composite" figure— the most important "personage" in *The Waste Land*, writes the poet in the notes he added to the poem—literally blind but figuratively capable of great insight; indeed, having lived— and participated—as both man and woman, he has the capac-ity to "foresee" all that happens between the on-fire "clerk carbuncular" and the indifferent "typist home at teatime" in the poem's geographically and thematically central section titled "The Fire Sermon"—the prophet thus participates liter-ally in the scene. "With dinner in mind," White records, this time, stopping in "an ex-speakeasy in East Fifty-third Street" (34), an echo with significant differences and outcome:

> From the next booth drifts the conversation of radio execu-tives; from the green salad comes the little taste of garlic. Behind me (eighteen inches...) a young intellectual is trying to persuade a girl to come live with him and be his love. She has her guard up, but he is extremely reasonable, careful not to overplay his hand. A combination of intellectual companion-ship and sexuality is what they have to offer each other, he feels. In the mirror over the bar I can see the ritual of the sec-ond drink. Then he has to go to the men's room and she has to go to the ladies' room, and when they return, the argument has lost its tone. And the fan takes over again, and the heat and the relaxed air and the memory of so many good little dinners in so many good little places, with the theme of love, the sound of ventilation, the brief medicinal illusion of gin. (34–35)

The single word "ritual" catches the repetition and recurrence, but White is less interested here than Eliot is in *The Waste Land* in any pattern that he as observer might perceive. White remains with the details, with the literal level, attentive, scru-pulous, *recording*. As he has (just) written, "New York pro-vides not only a continuing excitation but also a spectacle that is continuing. I wander around, re-examining this spectacle, hoping that I can put it on paper" (32).

Early on in *Here Is New York*, White plants the seed that he will bring to fruition in the course of the essay, referring to "this fragile participation in destiny," observed in the "link with Oz" thanks to the regular appearance of the actor Fred Stone at a shared lunch counter: a "man sitting next to me (about eighteen inches away along the wall)" (12). What White then terms "the gift of privacy with the excitement of participation" marks this particular experience and, by means of its "blend" of difference and opposition, defines New Yorkers (13). No one moment in the City, says White, is completely alone or separate: "I heard the *Queen Mary* blow one midnight,...and the sound carried the whole history of departure and longing and loss" (14).

The familiar essay itself, especially as White performs it, participates in the action and experience White so well describes, and embodies. *Here Is New York* is, in some ways, unusual for him as essayist. Certainly it begins less concretely, more reflectively, more philosophically perhaps, and less personally than do his other achievements in essay form. Yet, before long, in paragraph after paragraph, White turns, naturally it seems, from the general to the personal, reversing, in fact, the typical essayistic procedure of proceeding to the general (and universal) in, through, and by means of the concrete, the particular, and the personal. White's subject, though, is not himself, but the city, and he is writing, not a personal, but a familiar essay. Still, he accounts for the city by literally putting himself in it: "I am, at the moment of writing this..." (30), "It is Saturday....I turn through West Forty-eighth Street...." (32); "I stare through the west windows at the Manufacturers Trust Company and at the red brick fronts on the north side of Ninth Street...." (38); "I head east along Rivington" (40)—a walker in the city, to borrow the title of Alfred Kazin's book about New York. The descriptions, by the way, could usefully, instructively be compared with T.S. Eliot's of the modern city in *The Waste Land*, for White too observes the filth, the ennui, the angst, the competitiveness, the indifference, the suffering. White too discerns pattern, but, he may be more capacious, able to see pattern without reducing direct, concrete experience and its details for the sake of generalities. In any case, White observes the universal in the particular, timelessness in time, meaning in experience— notice, here, how he puts the reader, too, in the position of *participant*, shifting to the second-person:

> Walk the Bowery under the El at night and all you feel is a sort of cold guilt. Touched for a dime, you try to drop the coin and not touch the hand, because the hand is dirty; you try to avoid the glance, because the glance accuses. This is not so much personal menace as universal—the cold menace of unresolved human suffering and poverty and the advanced stages of the disease alcoholism. (38–39)

White knows, understands, and sympathizes, for "each sleeper" he sees, on the street, has "drained his release" (39). You (too) participate, even at a distance: be it as reader, at 18 inches from a fellow diner, or in giving alms, however minimal and with whatever contrivance and avoidance of physical contact. Moreover, the essay, as form, the pattern that White dramatically represents, takes you through the particular to the general and the universal, revealing in the process the extra-ordinary in the ordinary.

Perhaps above all else, New York provides its citizens something that is itself extraordinary and yet familiar if not precisely ordinary: "the city makes up for its hazards and its deficiencies by supplying its citizens with massive doses of a supplementary vitamin: the sense of belonging to something unique, cosmopolitan, mighty, and unparalleled" (26). All this the commuter misses—"the queerest bird of all" (18). He, simply put, does not *participate*:

> The suburb [the commuter] inhabits has no essential vitality of its own and is a mere roost where he comes at day's end to go to sleep. Except in rare cases, the man who lives in Mamaroneck or Little Neck or Teaneck, and works in New York, discovers nothing much about the city except the time of arrival and

departure of trains and buses, and the path to a quick lunch. He is desk-bound, and has never, idly roaming in the gloaming, stumbled suddenly on Belvedere Tower in the Park, seen the ramparts rise sheer from the water of the pond, and the boys along the shore fishing for minnows, girls stretched out negligently on the shelves of the rocks; he has never come suddenly on anything at all in New York as a loiterer, because he has had no time between trains. (19)

So described, the commuter appears as a familiar essayist's opposite. White continues his excursus:

He has fished in Manhattan's wallet and dug out coins but has never listened to Manhattan's breathing, never awakened to its morning, never dropped off to sleep in its night. About 400,000 men and women come charging onto the Island each week-day morning, out of the mouths of tubes and tunnels. Not many among them have ever spent a drowsy afternoon in the great rustling oaken silence of the reading room of the Public Library, with the book elevator (like an old water wheel) spewing out books onto the trays. They tend their furnaces in Westchester and in Jersey, but have never seen the furnaces of the Bowery, the fires that burn in oil drums on zero winter nights. They may work in the financial district downtown and never see the extravagant plantings of Rockefeller Center—the daffodils and grape hyacinths and birches and the flags trimmed to the wind on a fine morning in spring. Or they may work in a midtown office and may let a whole year swing round without sighting Governors Island from the sea wall. The commuter dies with tremendous mileage to his credit, but he is no rover. His entrances and exits are more devious than those in a prairie-dog village, and he calmly plays bridge while buried in the mud at the bottom of the East River. The Long Island Rail Road alone carried forty million commuters last year, but many of them were the same fellow retracing his steps. (19–21)

To this essentially satirical observation and description, White adds an unusually short paragraph, still thinking of the commuter but now offering an alternative, or perhaps it is an antidote, properly but differently represented by a particular and specific person, one named, at that:

> The terrain of New York is such that a resident sometimes travels farther, in the end, than a commuter. Irving Berlin's journey from Cherry Street in the lower East Side to an apartment uptown was through an alley and was only three or four miles in length; but it was like going three times around the world. (21)

It is hard, very hard, for a commuter to participate—in communion.

White may not exactly offer his readers communion. He does, at least, invite us into his world via his agreeable, and often accommodating, writing. This is no self-centered or egoistic act, no matter how much the modest and humble essayist insists that it is, refusing to aggrandize even the form that he obviously cherishes—and serves.

Very few (if any) religious images occur in White's essays, very little mention of religion in any shape or form at all. He does not so much eschew religious images as find neither place nor need of them. Andy White would likely even reject the label of layman that I propose for him. Would he also deny the presence of religious feelings in his essays? However that may be, and no one can be sure, his essays share both religious concerns and Christian perceptions. The very notion of "religious feeling without religious images" participates in the post-Reformation pattern of response that we have been tracing. The religious is alive and well.

7

RELIGIO CRITICAE: AN ESSAY ON RECEPTION AND RESPONSE

In many ways, T.S. Eliot's last great poem, *Four Quartets*, inverts his earlier great poem *The Waste Land*, replacing—not least in style of writing—fragmentariness, separation, discon- nection, and unrootedness with "association," "matrimonie," "daunsinge," mutual support, and (simple and unfamiliar) relations. *Four Quartets* stands as a tour de force, with perhaps even the potential to overcome the individual reader's "disso- ciation of sensibility," certainly involving her or him with the poet in establishing that "complete consort" that makes for recognition that no moment in the poem is "unattended" and no point in life identical, individual, separate, and uncon- nected. Not only does a "lifetime burn in every moment," but, just as *Four Quartets* "intersects" *The Waste Land*, meaning always, everywhere "intersects" experience.

I offer this last essay as a (further) expression of the critic's faith. A half century ago and a bit more, the poet David Gascoyne rendered a *Religio Poetae*, I doubt very much with the "layman's faiths" in mind. By "Religio Criticae" here, I mean especially *my* faith—I think of Dryden, in his *Religio Laici*: "If *Others* in the *same Glass better* see / 'Tis for *Themselves* they look, but not for *me:* / For *MY* Salvation must its Doom receive / Not from what *OTHERS*, but what *I* believe" (301–4).[1] I also mean somewhat more, for I suggest, if not a universal, a generalizable (and therefore essayistic) value to this memoirist *essai*.

As to my own *critical faith*, I can do little better than point to the young poet Alexander Pope, writing in *An Essay on*

Criticism and offering a brilliant account of the ideal critic. Pope obviously wonders if such a critic as he describes actually exists, or can; I cannot but wonder the same. However that may be, I retain, at the end of my career, the hope, and the belief, that many of the qualities enumerated here *do* exist in critics and always will—as long as we keep alive the possibility and the necessity.

> But where's the Man, who Counsel *can* bestow,
> Still *pleas'd* to *teach*, and yet not *proud* to *know?*
> Unbiass'd, or by *Favour* or by *Spite*;
> Not *dully prepossest*, nor *blindly right*;
> Tho' Learn'd, well-bred; and tho' well-bred, sincere;
> Modestly bold, and Humanly severe?
> Who to a *Friend* his Faults can freely show,
> And gladly praise the Merit of a *Foe?*
> Blest with a *Taste* exact, yet unconfin'd;
> A *Knowledge* both of *Books* and *Humankind*;
> *Gen'rous Converse*; a *Soul* exempt from *Pride*;
> And *Love to Praise*, with *Reason* on his Side? (631–42)[2]

You would be hard pressed to find a better description of the critical enterprise than *"Gen'rous Converse"* or a more inspiriting account of the critic—earlier in the essay-poem, Pope warned us not to let the man be lost in the critic—than the capaciousness here represented. Clearly, Pope subscribes to the notion of "association" of apparent opposites, and even if his texture feels somewhat less elastic than brittle, more schematic than imaginative and natural, there is more here than a hint of that "bridging of contradictory qualities" that drew Eliot's attention and praise. And even if Pope's "concordia discors" seems attenuated compared with the seventeenth-century Divines' capacity for the "yoking together of opposites" that "seems nearly impossible to the modern mind," a positive relation yet exists with Eliot and, say, Lancelot Andrewes.[3]

In the passage I have quoted from *An Essay on Criticism*, Pope is interested exclusively, it seems, in *moral response*—thus he warns, elsewhere in the poem, that we not lose the man in the critic (523). I agree that criticism is a moral act, but that kind of response is but one of many available to reading. Before response, in any case, or so it seems, there must be reception. To wit: Geoffrey Hartman has offered William Butler Yeats's famous "Leda and the Swan" as "a fable of the hermeneutic situation."[4] Hartman stresses there the strangeness in Leda's reception of the god. Later in the same book, *Criticism in the Wilderness*, Hartman represents "The Boy of Winander" passage in Wordsworth's *The Prelude* (Book 5) as a virtual allegory of reading: the boy—that is, the poet—is described as "[blowing] mimic hootings to the silent owls, / That they might answer him."[5] The owls prove "Responsive to his call," and so a situation of "demand and response" is set up in a way that directly recalls that of reading. Hartman's interest lies in the psychology of the moment, but I find in both examples, from Yeats as well as from Wordsworth, inklings (at least) of the analogy between the religious situation and that of reading and criticism.[6]

Pope does not say, nor Eliot, nor Hartman for that matter, that the critical act consists of at least two related parts. I mean, *reception* and *response*. Indeed, every act of responsible reading, whether performed by "common" readers or so-called professionals, consists of reception and response. Ordinarily, we separate them, as seems logical. But it is logical actually only in the way that Wordsworth himself means when, separating, or dissociating, he famously describes poetry as "emotion recollected in tranquillity": first, he says, comes the experience, then reflection on it, and only then, time having intervened, the poem. Eliot, of course, challenged Wordsworth, beginning in "Tradition and the Individual Talent," and a bit later, in "The Metaphysical Poets," he posited a "dissociation of sensibility" as having "set in" during the course of the seventeenth century, which effectively separated thinking and feeling and, from his point of view, essentially ruined poetry (turning it, via reflection, into essaying—the Romantic labelled his and Coleridge's revolutionary *Lyrical Ballads* "short essays").[7] In the instance of reception and response, it is impossible to state that response simply follows reception, for it is (also) involved in, and is a part of, reception.

Put in terms of reception-response, and with "Leda and the Swan" in mind, the situation of reading, and of criticism, must, I suggest, recall the receiving of God by the Virgin, which results in the birth of Jesus the Christ: Being fertilizes and impregnates Understanding (which is, of course, both Mary and the God-Man). Criticism thus completes reading, reception both requiring and leading to response. As Hartman has acknowledged, "the difference that reading makes is, most generally, writing."[8]

We appear to have arrived at a destination unsought by today's students. Like E.B. White, and Henry David Thoreau behind him, they may *believe*, but theirs is a noninstitutional, nondogmatic sort of faith: "religious feeling" perhaps but "without religious images."[9] They thus may represent the culmination of layman's faiths. But they should beware, for their spirit-ualism, evident all about us, from Evangelicalism to "New Age," is revealed by at least some of the laity we have treated as highly suspect and even radically dangerous. Dryden, for one, sought to bring together lay freedom with a religious, moral, and civic responsibility that forswore the abuses and the tyranny of the "private Spirit." His kind of capaciousness involves that highly desirable "bridging of contradictory qualities."

The prominence of this spirit-ualism exists alongside, and is to a considerable degree responsible for, the decline of Christianity in our time. The *spiritual*—disembodied, Gnostic, and Manichean at the core—is the Devil's province in these days. Eliot was right, after all, perhaps thinking of mid-seventeenth-century perversions, as Dryden would surely confirm: "the spirit killeth."[10] In E.B. White's terms, in other words, which he applied to Henry David Thoreau, there is abundant "religious feeling without religious images." When immanence is separated from transcendence, as when body and spirit are dissociated, Christianity suffers. Without Incarnation, there *is* no Christianity, our world given over to Manicheanism and Gnosticism unawares. Christianity is simply inseparable from the "bridging of contradictory qualities"— indeed, it is defined by and as precisely that.

That being so, we have perhaps renewed understanding of the relation of literature and Christianity.

Does religion, then, need literature?

In his well-known essay "Religion and Literature," T.S. Eliot wrote that "Literary criticism should be completed by criticism from a definite ethical and theological standpoint."[11] This position itself both stems from and parallels Eliot's earlier understanding, manifest in *The Sacred Wood*, that the critic must approach desired cultural critique indirectly, beginning, that is, with literature and proceeding in, through, and by means of it. Indirectness holds the key, for all our desire for immediacy (and, Derrida would say, *presence*). Behind that recognition, or at least parallel with it, is the Incarnational pattern. That means that you neither stop your journey with literature, nor once you have reached religion do you leave literature—the text, the literal, immanence—behind.

If Eliot is right in defining the relation of literature and *religion*, and I think he is, literature finds its completion in religion, and if I am right, Incarnational defines the relation of literature and *Christianity*. That is, the path thereto leads in, through, and by means of texts and the reading of them, secular as well as sacred.

Is literary study, then, a pastoral function and thus a necessary preparation for Christian understanding? In my case, at least, the structure of my "faith" reflects a process Incarnational in nature and texture. I have come, now, and at last, to the point of recognition, as well as of reception. I have written here, therefore, in this book, that is, as one who professes Christianity, one who, moreover, is essentially *un-Churched*. My past is, as I have said, Southern Baptist, my "letter," though, for some 20 years at the local Congregational Church, with which I feel no more allegiance. My heart and soul lie with Anglo-Catholicism, as is no doubt clear, although I have taken no formal steps toward it. It is surely of some consequence that, with Eliot, I have found that "Catholic Christianity...account[s] most satisfactorily for the world and especially the moral world within."[12] Insofar as I argue in this book, I do so, in the spirit of the essay or so I have intended, from without, rather than from a perspective inside that position. While I do not claim objectivity—nor have I sought any—I follow the layman's faith tradition in avoiding sectarianism and (at least that sort of) partiality.

As with so many others nowadays, and with many laymen across the centuries, institutionalization sticks in my craw. Perhaps I resist commitment, perhaps the formal giving (up) of myself, the public acknowledgment of my own incapacities alongside my pledge to *communicate*—and take certain responsibilities, to act, in other words, as well as to believe, say, and profess. It may ultimately be a question of *submission*— Eliot again: "Do not let me hear / Of the wisdom of old men, but rather of their folly, / Their fear of fear and frenzy, *their fear of possession, / Of belonging to another, or to God*" (*East Coker*). In short, I recognize that I have not completed the course, the journey of faith with its imposing and demanding structure.

We should not forget that the idea of binding, tying, and fastening lies deep within the word *religio* (which T.S. Eliot incarnates in his greatest poem), nor that Communion means an act of sharing, an act of participation, reception and response brought together.

Four Quartets thus lingers in the mind, connecting, and *requiring that we connect*. Here, recall, the fifth and final section of each of the four poems treats variously matters of writing. *Burnt Norton* readily acknowledges the slipperiness of words: they inevitably "strain, / Crack and sometimes break, under the burden," which is inseparable from "the tension," which means that they also "slip, slide, perish, / Decay with imprecision, will not stay in place, / Will not stay still."[13] As Sister Benedicta Ward has written, the Divines of the seventeenth century, especially, were "eager to link right praying with right action," particularly in the sphere of "their concern with words. . . . The relationship between grammar and theology is something of great importance for the Church. . . ."[14] Not surprisingly, then, Eliot returns to words themselves in *Little Gidding* drawing *Four Quartets* to a close. Here, now,

he brings "the old and the new" together in "An easy com-
merce," sounding an eloquent and powerful response to modes
of individualism, connecting with the important passage in
East Coker concerning "coniunction," "association," and
"concorde," all instances of a "commodious sacrament." The
emphasis falls, at poem's end, on mutuality, participation,
and communion so that, in writing too, the aim is for "every
word [to be] at home, / Taking its place to support the
others"—submission and participation. Common-ness is said
to exist "without vulgarity" just as formality and precision
exist without "pedantry."[15] In short, echoing the Elizabethan
rustics dancing around an open fire depicted in *East Coker*,
Eliot lauds and advocates "The complete consort dancing
together."

That Eliot closes each of *Four Quartets* with scrupulous
attention to words and writing, the difficulty, the responsibility, and the opportunity, of course matters. That attention not
only links him to Anglicanism and especially the seventeenth-
century Divines whom he so admired, but it also points ineluc-
tably to the relationship between writing and action, literature
and religion. Acting in life and writing, we are entitled to
conclude, are analogues one of another, as are laity, amateur,
common reader, and essayist. As analogues, they participate—
commune—in and share a pattern.

As I once wrote, without, I hope, overdramatizing, my life
changed the day I (re)discovered "the glorious essay" (*Antioch
Review*). By means of the essay, I have come to appreciate tension, itself a corollary of the *via media* that is the form. In my
case, at least, the lessons of the essay may not be separated
from those rendered by Old Possum, especially to grasp the
notion of Incarnation as pattern, that "figure in the carpet"
that must interest all students of literature. I mean, both "pattern" and "Incarnation," for those of us in literary studies read
"comparatively and laterally," attending to repetitions and resonances, and we study texts that themselves represent forms of
embodiment.

NOTES

PREFATORY ESSAY

1. The commentary on literature and religion is extensive, including the excellent collections *Religion and Modern Literature: Essays in Theory and Criticism,* ed. G.B. Tennyson and Edward Ericson, Jr. (Grand Rapids, MI: Eerdmans, 1975), which includes the important essays by T.S. Eliot and J. Hillis Miller, among others, and *Religion and Literature: A Reader,* ed. Robert Detweiler and David Jasper (Louisville, KY: Westminster John Knox, 2005). See also Helen Gardner, *Religion and Literature* (London: Faber and Faber, 1971). My own earlier writings include "Dehellenizing Literary Criticism," *College English,* 41 (1980), 769–79, and "A(fter) D(econstruction): Literature and Religion in the Wake of Deconstruction," *Studies in the Literary Imagination,* 18 (1985), 89–100.
2. Ezra Pound, *ABC of Reading* (New York: New Directions, 1950).
3. See Rowan Williams, *Grace and Necessity: Reflections on Art and Love* (Harrisburg, PA: Morehouse, 2005).
4. T.S. Eliot, *Ash-Wednesday* (New York: Harcourt, Brace, 1930).
5. Ezra Pound, "I Gather the Limbs of Osiris," *Selected Prose, 1909–1965,* ed. William Cookson (New York: New Directions, 1975), 21.
6. I have discussed this "tradition" in *The Faith of John Dryden: Change and Continuity* (Lexington: University Press of Kentucky, 1980).
7. Christopher Hill, *The World Turned Upside Down: Radical Ideas during the English Revolution* (New York: Viking, 1972).
8. See my *Tracing the Essay: Through Experience to Meaning* (Athens: University of Georgia Press, 2005) and *Reading Essays: An Invitation* (Athens: University of Georgia Press, 2008).
9. John Dryden, *Poems and Fables,* ed. James Kinsley (London: Oxford University Press, 1962).

10. Jacques Derrida, "Living On: Border Lines," trans. James Hulbert, in *Deconstruction and Criticism*, by Harold Bloom, Paul de Man, Jacques Derrida, Geoffrey Hartman, and J. Hillis Miller (New York: Seabury Press, 1979).
11. Alexander Pope, *Poetry and Prose*, ed. Aubrey Williams (Boston: Riverside-Houghton Mifflin, 1969).
12. Maynard Mack, introduction, The Twickenham Edition of *The Poems of Alexander Pope: An Essay on Man*, ed. Mack (New Haven, CT: Yale University Press, 1950).
13. Cid Corman, *The Faith of Poetry* (Guilford, VT: Longhouse, 1989).
14. Ibid., 1.
15. Ibid.
16. Peter Gizzi, *The Outernationale* (Middletown, CT: Wesleyan University Press, 2008).
17. Corman, 7; italics added.
18. Andrew Lytle, preface, *The Hero with the Private Parts* (Baton Rouge: Louisiana State University Press, 1966), xx. I have discussed "writing-as-reading" in *Reading Essays*, especially 1–17 and 260–67.
19. Cynthia Ozick, "Metaphor and Memory," *Metaphor and Memory* (New York: Knopf, 1989), 279.

INTRODUCTION: "THE HINT HALF GUESSED, THE GIFT HALF UNDERSTOOD"

1. T.S. Eliot, *Four Quartets* (New York: Harcourt, Brace, 1943).
2. T.S. Eliot, "The *Pensées* of Pascal," *Selected Essays*, 3rd ed. (London: Faber and Faber, 1951), 408.
3. Flannery O'Connor, *Mystery and Manners* (New York: Farrar, Straus and Giroux, 1969), 66. See my *Tracing the Essay: Through Experience to Meaning* (Athens: University of Georgia Press, 2005).
4. Quoted in *The Art of the Personal Essay*, ed. Phillip Lopate (New York: Anchor-Doubleday, 1995), xxxvii.
5. Herbert N. Schneidau, *Sacred Discontent: The Bible and Western Tradition* (Baton Rouge: Louisiana State University Press, 1976), 49.
6. William J. Harvey, *The Art of George Eliot* (London: Chatto and Windus, 1961).

7. G.K. Chesterton, "A Piece of Chalk," in Lopate, ed., *The Art of the Personal Essay*, 249–52.

8. Robert Browning, "Fra Lippo Lippi," in M.H. Abrams et al., eds., *The Norton Anthology of English Literature*, 6th ed. (New York: Norton, 1993), vol. 2.

9. Louis Menand, *Revising Modernism: T.S. Eliot and His Context* (New York: Oxford University Press, 1986), 126.

10. Quoted in Ezra Pound, *Selected Prose 1909–1965*, ed. William Cookson (New York: New Directions, 1975), 9.

11. Ibid. Cookson quotes Pound's *Terra Italica* (1932).

12. F. Scott Fitzgerald, "The Crack-Up," *The Crack-Up*, ed. Edmund Wilson (New York: New Directions, 1945), 69; James Baldwin, "Notes of a Native Son," *Notes of a Native Son* (Boston: Beacon Press, 1955), 113.

13. T.S. Eliot, "The Metaphysical Poets," *Selected Essays*, 287.

14. T.S. Eliot, "Andrew Marvell," ibid., 303.

15. T.S. Eliot, *The Sacred Wood* (London: Methuen, 1920), 33.

16. Ibid., 45.

17. Ibid., 28.

18. Ibid., xi–xii.

19. Eliot, *Selected Essays*, 388.

20. James Joyce, *A Portrait of the Artist as a Young Man*, ed. Chester G. Anderson (New York: Viking, 1968), 221.

21. T.S. Eliot, "Baudelaire in Our Time," *Essays Ancient and Modern* (London: Faber and Faber, 1936), 66n.

22. C.H. Sisson, "Sevenoaks Essays," *The Avoidance of Literature: Collected Essays* (Manchester: Carcanet, 1978).

23. Pound, "The Wisdom of Poetry," in *Selected Prose 1909–1965*, 361–62.

24. Vincent E. Miller, "Eliot's Submission to Time," *Sewanee Review*, 84 (1976), 448–64.

1   ESSAYING THE *VIA MEDIA*: JOHN DRYDEN'S *RELIGIO LAICI* AND ALEXANDER POPE'S *AN ESSAY ON MAN*

1. The commendatory poems are reprinted in the California Edition of *The Works of John Dryden: Poems 1681–1684*, ed. H.T. Swedenberg, Jr. (Berkeley: University of California Press, 1972), 475–78.

2. John Dryden, *Poems and Fables,* ed. James Kinsley (London: Oxford University Press, 1962). All quotations of Dryden's poems come from this edition.

3. Alexander Pope, *Poetry and Prose,* ed. Aubrey Williams (Boston: Riverside-Houghton Mifflin, 1969). All quotations of Pope's poems come from this edition, unless otherwise indicated.

4. I elaborate on this minor tradition in *The Faith of John Dryden: Change and Continuity* (Lexington: University Press of Kentucky, 1980).

5. On these points, see my *Tracing the Essay: Through Experience to Meaning* (Athens: University of Georgia Press, 2005).

6. For the religious and political backgrounds, see my book cited above, as well as "Dryden's *Religio Laici*: A Reappraisal," *Studies in Philology,* 75 (1978), 347–70. In both places, I appraise at some length earlier treatments of Dryden's poem and of his evolving religious understanding.

7. Aubrey Williams, introduction, The Twickenham Edition of *The Poems of Alexander Pope*: *Pastoral Poetry and "An Essay on Criticism"* (New Haven, CT: Yale University Press, 1961).

8. See my "Poetic Strategies in *An Essay on Criticism,* Lines 201–559," *South Atlantic Bulletin,* 44 (1979), 43–47.

9. T.S. Eliot, "Baudelaire in Our Time," *Essays Ancient and Modern* (London: Faber and Faber, 1936), 66n.

10. Alexander Pope, "The Universal Prayer," The Twickenham Edition of *The Poems of Alexander Pope*: *Minor Poems,* ed. Norman Ault and John Butt (London: Methuen, 1964).

2   "A grander scheme of salvation than the chryst\<e\>ain religion": John Keats, a New Religion of Love, and the Hoodwinking of "The Eve of St. Agnes"

1. *The Letters of John Keats,* ed. Hyder E. Rollins (Cambridge, MA: Harvard University Press), 2.70–71, 115.

2. Quoted in Robert Gittings, *John Keats* (London: Heinemann, 1968), 425. As Gittings notes, Keats omitted some potentially offensive oaths from the mouths of Madeline and Porphyro, while retaining that in line 145.

3. *Letters* 2.304. The text used throughout for the poems is *Keats: Poetical Works,* ed. H.W. Garrod (1956; rpt. London: Oxford University Press, 1966).

4. Ibid., 2.80, 2.101–2.
5. Ibid., 2.101–2.
6. Ibid., 2.102.
7. Ibid.
8. Ibid., 2.103.
9. Ibid., 1.179.
10. Hugh Miller, *Essays* (London, 1856–62), 1.452; William Michael Rossetti, *Life of John Keats* (London, 1887), 183.
11. Earl Wasserman, *The Finer Tone: Keats' Major Poems* (Baltimore, MD: Johns Hopkins Press, 1953).
12. Jack Stillinger, "The Hoodwinking of Madeline: Scepticism in 'The Eve of St. Agnes,'" *Studies in Philology*, 58 (1961), 533–55.
13. The present essay modifies my original "*The Eve of St. Agnes* Re-Considered," *Tennessee Studies in Literature*, 18 (1973), 113–32. See also Stuart M. Sperry, Jr., "Romance as Wish-Fulfillment: Keats's *The Eve of St. Agnes*," *Studies in Romanticism*, 10 (1971), 27–42.
14. I take this notion from the highly suggestive book by Walter A. Davis, *The Act of Interpretation: A Critique of Literary Reason* (Chicago: University of Chicago Press, 1978).
15. *Letters*, 2.163.
16. James D. Boulger, "Keats' Symbolism," *ELH*, 28 (1961), 258–59.
17. *Letters*, 2.223–24.
18. Ibid., 81.

3   George Eliot's "Layman's Faith": The Lyrical Essay-Novel *Adam Bede*

1. William J. Harvey argues, however, that Eliot so constructs the story—narrative and commentary—as to engage the reader directly, *entangling* us, complexifying our response. It requires some effort, however, to convince oneself, let alone others, of Eliot's masterful technique and rhetorical strategy, although many have tried. See *The Art of George Eliot* (London: Chatto and Windus, 1961).
2. For the reader's convenience, given the large number of quotations from the novel, I have given page numbers thusly; they are to *Adam Bede* (New York: Signet-New American Library, 1961).
3. William Wordsworth, Preface to *Lyrical Ballads*, in M.H. Abrams et al., eds., *The Norton Anthology of English Literature*, 6th ed. (New York: Norton, 1993), 2.144.

158   NOTES

4. Donald Davie, *These the Companions* (Cambridge: Cambridge University Press, 1982).
5. Cynthia Ozick, *Metaphor and Memory* (New York: Knopf, 1989), 278
6. Quoted in ibid., 279.
7. Ibid.
8. Cynthia Ozick, "The Riddle of the Ordinary," in Lydia Fakundiny, ed., *The Art of the Essay* (Boston: Houghton Mifflin, 1991), 421.

4   PRIESTS OF ETERNAL IMAGINATION: LITERATURE AND RELIGION—THE INSTANCE OF JAMES JOYCE AND *A PORTRAIT OF THE ARTIST AS A YOUNG MAN*

1. The text of the novel used throughout is James Joyce, *A Portrait of the Artist as a Young Man*, ed. Chester G. Anderson (New York: Viking, 1968). For the reader's convenience, I include all page references thusly.
2. See Wayne C. Booth, *The Rhetoric of Fiction* (Chicago: University of Chicago Press, 1961).
3. Anderson, 520 n., in Joyce, *A Portrait*.
4. Anderson, 521 n., in ibid.
5. John Dryden, *Poems and Fables*, ed. James Kinsley (Oxford: Oxford University Press, 1962).
6. Alexander Pope, *Poetry and Prose*, ed. Aubrey Williams (Boston: Riverside-Houghton Mifflin, 1969).
7. Maynard Mack, introduction, The Twickenham Edition of *The Poems of Alexander Pope: An Essay on Man*, ed. Mack (London: Methuen, 1950), lxxvii.
8. Hugh Kenner, "In the Wake of the Anarch," *Gnomon: Essays on Contemporary Literature* (New York: McDowell, Obolensky, 1958), 176.
9. M.H. Abrams, *Natural Supernaturalism: Tradition and Revolution in Romantic Literature* (New York: Norton, 1971).
10. William Wordsworth, *The Prelude*, in M.H. Abrams et al., eds., *The Norton Anthology of English Literature*, 6th ed. (New York: Norton, 1993), 2.144.
11. Ezra Pound, "Credo," in *Selected Prose 1909–65*, ed. William Cookson (New York: New Directions, 1975), 53.
12. Pound, "Axiomata," in ibid., 49.

13. Pound, "*Deus et Amor*," in ibid., 70.
14. Ibid.
15. Pound, "*Religio* or, The Child's Guide to Knowledge," in ibid., 47.
16. Peter Makin, *Bunting: The Shaping of His Verse* (Oxford: Clarendon Press, 1992), 202. In footnote 42 on page 202, Makin identifies the sources of his quotations.
17. T.S. Eliot, *Four Quartets* (New York: Harcourt, Brace, 1943).
18. Vincent Sherry, *The Uncommon Tongue: The Poetry and Criticism of Geoffrey Hill* (Ann Arbor: University of Michigan Press, 1987), 25.
19. Ibid., 21.
20. Geoffrey Hill, quoted in ibid.
21. Ibid.
22. Ibid., 22.
23. Sherry, 22. The quotation is, according to Sherry, a description offered by Joseph Cary in *Three Modern Italian Poets* (New York: New York University Press, 1969).
24. Geoffrey Hill, *The Mystery of the Charity of Charles Péguy* (London: Andre Deutsch, 1983), 31.

5   Journey toward Understanding:
T.S. Eliot and the Progress of
the "Intelligent Believer"

1. T.S. Eliot, preface, *For Lancelot Andrewes: Essays on Style and Order* (London: Faber and Gwyer, 1928), ix.
2. T.S. Eliot, "The *Pensées* of Pascal," *Selected Essays*, 3rd ed. (London: Faber and Faber, 1951), 411.
3. See Lyndall Gordon, *T.S. Eliot: An Imperfect Life* (New York: Norton, 2000).
4. T.S. Eliot, "The *Pensées* of Pascal," *Selected Essays*, 411.
5. Ibid., 412.
6. Ibid., 411.
7. Ibid., 408.
8. Alexander Pope, *The Dunciad* (4.471) in *Poetry and Prose*, ed. Aubrey Williams (Boston: Riverside-Houghton Mifflin, 1969).
9. For a number of reasons, not least the rhetorical value of keeping in mind the intersection of whole and part, I will read

Four Quartets in the four individual and separate editions, all published by Faber and Faber: *Burnt Norton* (1941), *East Coker* (1940), *The Dry Salvages* (1941), and *Little Gidding* (1942). All four were published together for the first time in 1943. See Helen Gardner, *The Composition of "Four Quartets"* (London: Faber and Faber, 1978).

10. See my forthcoming study *T.S. Eliot and the Essay* (Waco, TX: Baylor University Press, 2010).
11. C.H. Sisson, *Anglican Essays* (Manchester: Carcanet, 1983).
12. T.S. Eliot, "Tradition and the Individual Talent," *The Sacred Wood* (London: Methuen, 1920), 28.
13. Ibid., 28–29.
14. Cynthia Ozick, "Metaphor and Memory," *Metaphor and Memory* (New York: Knopf, 1989), 279.

6 "RELIGIOUS FEELING WITHOUT RELIGIOUS IMAGES": E.B. WHITE'S ESSAYS AND THE POETICS OF PARTICIPATION

1. E.B. White, *Essays* (New York: Harper and Row, 1977), 235. Page references as here are given in the text for the reader's convenience.
2. John Dryden, *Poems and Fables*, ed. James Kinsley (London: Oxford University Press), 1962.
3. Quoted in Marie Cabaud Meaney, *Simone Weil's Apologetic Use of Literature: Her Christological Interpretation of Greek Texts* (Oxford: Oxford University Press, 2007), 5.
4. Ibid., vii.
5. Ibid., 18.
6. Ibid., 201.
7. Ibid., 210.
8. T.S. Eliot, *The Dry Salvages* (London: Faber and Faber, 1941).
9. T.S. Eliot, *Little Gidding* (London: Faber and Faber, 1942).
10. T.S. Eliot, *The Sacred Wood* (London: Methuen, 1920), 18.
11. T.S. Eliot, *Selected Essays*, 3rd ed. (London: Faber and Faber, 1951), 408.
12. *Tracing the Essay: Through Experience to Meaning* (Athens: University of Georgia Press, 2005).
13. Cynthia Ozick, *Metaphor and Memory* (New York: Knopf, 1989), 279.

14. Richard Selzer, "A Worm from My Notebook," in Lydia Fakundiny, ed., *The Art of the Essay* (Boston: Houghton Mifflin, 1991), 435. I have written about this essay at some length in *Reading Essays: An Invitation* (Athens: University of Georgia Press, 2008), 159–66.

15. Paul H. Fry, *The Reach of Criticism: Method and Perception in Literary Theory* (New Haven, CT: Yale University Press, 1983), 200.

16. See Joseph Epstein, *A Line Out for a Walk: Familiar Essays* (New York: Norton, 1991).

17. I discuss "Death of a Pig" at length in *Tracing the Essay.*

18. It is this book from which I have taken all quotations of *Here Is New York* (New York: Harper and Brothers, 1949), with page references provided in text. I discuss this essay at some length in *On the Familiar Essay: Challenging Academic Orthodoxies* (New York: Palgrave Macmillan, 2009).

7   *RELIGIO CRITICAE*: AN ESSAY ON RECEPTION AND RESPONSE

1. John Dryden, *Poems and Fables*, ed. James Kinsley (London: Oxford University Press, 1962).

2. Alexander Pope, *Poetry and Prose*, ed. Aubrey Williams (Boston: Riverside-Houghton Mifflin, 1969).

3. Adam Nicolson, *God's Secretaries: The Making of the King James Bible* (New York: HarperCollins, 2003), 33.

4. Geoffrey H. Hartman, *Criticism in the Wilderness: The Study of Literature Today* (New Haven, CT: Yale University Press, 1980), 35.

5. Quoted in ibid., 221.

6. Ibid., 221.

7. William Wordsworth, Preface to *Lyrical Ballads*, in M.H. Abrams et al., eds., *The Norton Anthology of English Literature*, 6th ed. (New York: Norton, 1993), 2.144.

8. Hartman, 19.

9. E.B. White, *Essays* (New York: Harper and Row, 1977), 235.

10. T.S. Eliot, *Essays Ancient and Modern* (London: Faber and Faber, 1936), 66n.

11. Ibid., 93.

12. T.S. Eliot, *Selected Essays*, 3rd ed. (London: Faber and Faber, 1951), 408.

13. T.S. Eliot, *Burnt Norton* (London: Faber and Faber, 1941).

14. Sister Benedicta Ward, introduction, *The Spirit of Holiness: An Introduction to Six Seventeenth-Century Anglican Writers.* By Richard Southern, Sister Benedicta Ward, Kathleen Lea, and Mary Chitty (Oxford: SLG Press, 1976), vii–viii.

15. T.S. Eliot, *Little Gidding* (London: Faber and Faber, 1942).

BIBLIOGRAPHY

Abrams, M.H. *Natural Supernaturalism: Tradition and Revolution in Romantic Literature.* New York: Norton, 1971.

Anderson, Chester G. *See* Joyce, James.

Atkins, G. Douglas. "A(fter) D(econstruction): Literature and Religion in the Wake of Deconstruction." *Studies in the Literary Imagination* 18 (1985), 89–100.

———. "Dehellenizing Literary Criticism." *College English* 41 (1980), 769–79.

———. "Dryden's *Religio Laici*: A Reappraisal." *Studies in Philology* 75 (1978), 347–70.

———. "*The Eve of St. Agnes* Reconsidered." *Tennessee Studies in Literature* 18 (1973), 113–32.

———. *The Faith of John Dryden: Change and Continuity.* Lexington: University Press of Kentucky, 1980.

———. *On the Familiar Essay: Challenging Academic Orthodoxies.* New York: Palgrave Macmillan, 2009.

———. "Poetic Strategies in *An Essay on Criticism*, Lines 201–559." *South Atlantic Bulletin* 44 (1979), 43–47.

———. *Reading Essays: An Invitation.* Athens: University of Georgia Press, 2008.

———. *Tracing the Essay: Through Experience to Meaning.* Athens: University of Georgia Press, 2005.

Baldwin, James. *Notes of a Native Son.* Boston: Beacon Press, 1955.

Booth, Wayne C. *The Rhetoric of Fiction.* Chicago: University of Chicago Press, 1961.

Boulger, James D. "Keats' Symbolism." *ELH* 28 (1961), 244–59.

Browning, Robert. "Fra Lippo Lippi." In *The Norton Anthology of English Literature.*

Chesterton, G.K. "A Piece of Chalk." In Lopate, ed., *The Art of the Personal Essay*, 249–52.

Corman, Cid. *The Faith of Poetry.* Guilford, VT: Longhouse, 1989.

———. *Livingdying.* New York: New Directions, 1970.

Davis, Walter A. *The Act of Interpretation: A Critique of Literary Reason*. Chicago: University of Chicago Press, 1978.

Derrida, Jacques. "Living On: Border Lines," trans. James Hulbert. In *Deconstruction and Criticism*, by Harold Bloom, Paul de Man, Jacques Derrida, Geoffrey Hartman, and J. Hillis Miller. New York: Seabury Press, 1979.

Detweiler, Robert, and David Jasper, eds. *Religion and Literature: A Reader*. Louisville, KY: Westminster John Knox, 2000.

Dryden, John. *Poems and Fables*. Ed. James Kinsley. London: Oxford University Press, 1962.

———. *Works* (California Edition): *Poems 1681–1684*. Ed. H.T. Swedenberg, Jr. Berkeley: University of California Press, 1972.

Eliot, George. *Adam Bede*. 1859. New York: Signet-New American Library, 1961.

Eliot, T.S. *Ash-Wednesday*. New York: Harcourt, Brace, 1930.

———. *The Dry Salvages*. London: Faber and Faber, 1941.

———. *Essays Ancient and Modern*. London: Faber and Faber, 1936.

———. *Four Quartets*. New York: Harcourt, Brace, 1943.

———. *Little Gidding*. London: Faber and Faber, 1942.

———. "Religion and Literature." In Tennyson.

———. *The Sacred Wood*. London: Methuen, 1920.

———. *Selected Essays*. 3rd ed. London: Faber and Faber, 1951.

Epstein, Joseph. *A Line Out for a Walk: Familiar Essays*. New York: Norton, 1991.

Fakundiny, Lydia, ed. *The Art of the Essay*. Boston: Houghton Mifflin, 1991.

Fitzgerald, F. Scott. *The Crack-Up*. Ed. Edmund Wilson. New York: New Directions, 1945.

Fry, Paul H. *The Reach of Criticism: Method and Perception in Literary Theory*. New Haven, CT: Yale University Press, 1983.

Gardner, Helen. *Religion and Literature*. London: Faber and Faber, 1971.

Gittings, Robert. *John Keats*. London: Heinemann, 1968.

Gizzi, Peter. *The Outernationale*. Middletown, CT: Wesleyan University Press, 2008.

Gordon, Lyndall. *T.S. Eliot: An Imperfect Life*. New York: Norton, 2000.

Harvey, William J. *The Art of George Eliot*. London: Chatto and Windus, 1961.

Hill, Christopher. *The World Turned Upside Down: Radical Ideas during the English Revolution*. New York: Viking, 1972.

Hill, Geoffrey. *The Mystery of the Charity of Charles Péguy.* London: Andre Deutsch, 1983.

Joyce, James. *A Portrait of the Artist as a Young Man.* Ed. Chester G. Anderson, 1916. New York: Viking, 1968.

Keats, John. *The Letters of John Keats.* Ed. Hyder E. Rollins. 2 vols. Cambridge, MA: Harvard University Press, 1958.

———. *Poetical Works.* Ed. H.W. Garrod. 1956. London: Oxford University Press, 1966.

Kenner, Hugh. *Gnomon: Essays on Contemporary Literature.* New York: McDowell, Obolensky, 1958.

Lytle, Andrew. *The Hero with the Private Parts.* Baton Rouge: Louisiana State University Press, 1966.

Mack, Maynard. Introduction. The Twickenham Edition of *The Poems of Alexander Pope: An Essay on Man.* Ed. Mack. New Haven, CT: Yale University Press, 1950.

Meaney, Marie Cabaud. *Simone Weil's Apologetic Use of Literature: Her Christological Interpretation of Greek Texts.* Oxford: Oxford University Press, 2007.

Menand, Louis. *Revising Modernism: T.S. Eliot and His Context.* New York: Oxford University Press, 1986.

Miller, Hugh. *Essays.* London, 1856. Vol. 1.

Miller, J. Hillis. "Literature and Religion." In *Relations of Literary Study: Essays on Interdisciplinary Contributions,* ed. James E. Thorpe. New York: Modern Language Association, 111–26.

O'Connor, Flannery. *Mystery and Manners.* New York: Farrar, Straus and Giroux, 1970.

Ozick, Cynthia. *Metaphor and Memory.* New York: Knopf, 1989.

———. "The Riddle of the Ordinary." In Fakundiny, 416–23.

Pope, Alexander. *Poetry and Prose.* Ed. Aubrey Williams. Boston: Riverside-Houghton Mifflin, 1969.

Pound, Ezra. *ABC of Reading.* London: Routledge, 1934.

———. *Selected Prose, 1909–1965.* Ed. William Cookson. New York: New Directions, 1975.

Rossetti, William Michael. *Life of John Keats.* London, 1887.

Schneidau, Herbert N. *Sacred Discontent: The Bible and Western Tradition.* Baton Rouge: Louisiana State University Press, 1976.

Selzer, Richard. "A Worm from My Notebook." In Fakundiny, 434–39.

Sherry, Vincent. *The Uncommon Tongue: The Poetry and Criticism of Geoffrey Hill.* Ann Arbor: University of Michigan Press, 1987.

Sisson, C.H. *Anglican Essays*. Manchester: Carcanet, 1983.

———. *The Avoidance of Literature: Collected Essays*. Manchester: Carcanet, 1978.

Sperry, Stuart M., Jr. "Romance as Wish-Fulfillment: Keats's *The Eve of St. Agnes*." *Studies in Romanticism* 10 (1971), 27–42.

Stillinger, Jack. "The Hoodwinking of Madeline: Scepticism in 'The Eve of St. Agnes,'" *Studies in Philology* 58 (1961), 533–55.

Tennyson, G.B., and Edward Ericson, Jr., eds. *Religion and Modern Literature: Essays in Theory and Criticism*. Grand Rapids, MI: Eerdmans, 1975.

Ward, Sister Benedicta. Introduction. *The Beauty of Holiness: An Introduction to Six Seventeenth-Century Anglican Writers*. By Richard Southern, Sister Benedicta Ward, Kathleen Lea, and Mary Chitty. Oxford: SLG Press, 1976, v–x.

Wasserman, Earl. *The Finer Tone: Keats' Major Poems*. Baltimore: Johns Hopkins Press, 1953.

White, E.B. *Essays*. New York: Harper and Row, 1977.

———. *Here Is New York*. New York: Harper and Brothers, 1949.

Williams, Aubrey. Introduction. The Twickenham Edition of *The Poems of Alexander Pope: Pastoral Poetry and "An Essay on Criticism."* Ed. Williams. New Haven, CT: Yale University Press, 1961.

Williams, Rowan. *Grace and Necessity: Reflections on Art and Love*. Harrisburg, PA: Morehouse, 2005.

Wordsworth, William. Preface to *Lyrical Ballads*. In *The Norton Anthology of English Literature*, 6th ed., ed. M.H. Abrams et al. New York: Norton, 1993. Vol. 2.

———. *The Prelude*. In *The Norton Anthology of English Literature*.

INDEX